Assessing older people's health and social needs
Qualitative research investigating health beliefs and social factors
relevant to older people's health

WESTON
COLLEGE
LIBRARY

Assessing older people's health and social needs

Qualitative research investigating health beliefs and social factors relevant to older people's health

Lin Fee, Ann Cronin, Rosemarie Simmons, Salma Choudry

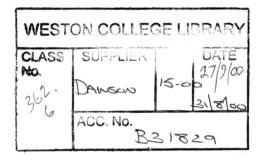
ISBN 0 7521 1502 2

© Health Education Authority 1999

Health Education Authority
Trevelyan House
30 Great Peter Street
London SW1P 2HW

www.hea.org.uk

Text composition Ken Brooks
Printed in Great Britain

Contents

Acknowledgements

We wish to thank the authors, Lin Fee, Ann Cronin, Rosemarie Simmons and Salma Choudry from the Surrey Social and Market Research (SSMR), Department of Sociology, University of Surrey, for having conducted this qualitative research. Thanks are also due to the following individuals and organisations for their assistance: Professor Sara Arber; Elaine Bowyer; Wendy Bye; Suzanne Cohen; Frank and Audrey Conroy; Jean Jackson MBE; Maureen Mason; John Sailsman, Nisa Sulaimani; Age Concern, County Durham, Leicester, Leicestershire, Newcastle-upon-Tyne, Portsmouth, Rutland, Surrey; 50+ Group, Taro Centre, Petersfield, Hants; 'Go Five-Oh', Surrey; Hampshire 'Meals on Wheels'; Quality Fieldwork, Birmingham; 'Well Being' Project, Surrey.

Authors of this report

Lin Fee
Ann Cronin
Rosemarie Simmons
Salma Choudry
Surrey Social and Market Research (SSMR),
Department of Sociology, University of Surrey

HEA Research Team

Seta Waller, *Research Manager*
Dominic McVey, *Head of Research*
Adam Crosier, *Senior Researcher*

Foreword

The health of older people has sometimes been treated as less important than that of younger people, either because older people are considered less productive or because ill health is deemed an inevitable consequence of later life. Furthermore, older people are often regarded as a homogeneous group, which in turn conceals inequalities in this population. With these issues in mind the HEA commissioned a number of research projects to highlight the diversity of older people's health needs and the health promotion issues relevant to later life. The first of these studies published by the HEA was a review entitled *Researching older people's health needs and health promotion issues*, and it examined the influence of the physical and social environment on older people's health and highlighted gaps in the current research literature. The second attempted to go beyond the basic descriptive analysis provided by many large-scale government surveys to look deeper into the data and examine the diversity within older populations. Four British datasets have been subjected to multivariate analysis looking at a range of issues including diet, smoking, alcohol consumption and physical activity to identify the characteristics shared by those most likely to engage in health damaging behaviour. The findings from this work are reported in the HEA publication *Health-related behaviour and attitudes of older people – a secondary analysis of national datasets*. The results from a third study entitled *Assessing older people's health and social needs* are presented in this report. This qualitatvie investigation was commissioned to examine in detail the social factors that influence older people's health beliefs and health promoting behaviour.

The aims of this study reflect the HEA's strategy of developing the knowledge base of health promotion, and all those concerned with the health and well being of older people will find in this report fresh and valuable insights into this diverse, under-researched and increasingly important population.

Dominic McVey
Head of Research
Health Education Authority

Executive summary

Introduction

In recent years, there has been an increase in interest in the health of older people. Policymakers and physicians recognise that the health expectancy of older people has not kept pace with increased life expectancy and a steady rise in the proportion of older people in the UK population. In the early years of the century, attention focused on eliminating 'diseases of poverty', such as diphtheria and tuberculosis, and on improving the survival chances of infants and children. At the end of the century, a far larger proportion of the health budget is devoted to providing health care for people aged 50 years and older.

In order to assist health providers and policymakers to anticipate need among older age-groups, extensive research has been carried out into the influence which social factors have on the types of illness experienced in older age. However, little is known about the social factors which influence older people's health beliefs and health-promoting behaviours. Although the category 'older people' spans two generations, Ginn, Arber and Cooper (1997) have noted that among both health providers and health researchers it is common to treat older people as a homogeneous group sharing similar health experiences and attitudes. However, this ignores the way in which social factors such as ethnicity, gender, class, marital status and geographical location affect life and work experiences which, in turn, affect health experiences, behaviours and attitudes.

The Health Education Authority (HEA) commissioned a study, using qualitative research methods, to examine the social factors which influence older people's health beliefs and health-promoting behaviours. The aims of the study reflect the HEA's strategy of developing the knowledge base of health promotion in order to promote the development of conditions in which people and communities can take control over their own health. The objectives of the research were to:

- explore beliefs and attitudes towards the concept of health
- examine attitudes towards health and social services
- assess the response to health promotion initiatives, in particular information and recommendations on improving health
- explore older people's self-perceptions of ageing and health
- identify older people's health concerns and how they relate to their own circumstances
- explore the perceptions of improving the quality of life
- identify perceptions of health promotion issues relevant to the target group.

Methodology

The study was carried out in two stages. The first stage consisted of 17 focus groups and the second stage involved 90 in-depth interviews. In both stages, attention was paid to ensuring that different sectors of the older population were represented in the research. While there was an emphasis on recruiting participants from socioeconomic groups C1, C2, D and E, care was taken to ensure that participants represented a wide range of ages and personal circumstances. Participants were divided into three age groups, that is, 55–64, 65–74, 75+, and the sample was selected to include the following:

- people living alone, with a spouse or partner, with relatives, or in a multi-generation family group
- people in 'good' and 'poor' health
- people with and without a disability
- carers and non-carers
- a mixture of social classes and ethnicity which reflects the composition of the wider population
- people living in their own homes, private or local authority rented accommodation, sheltered or warden-assisted accommodation, and residential care.

Stage 1: Focus groups

The use of focus groups is a particularly appropriate method for collecting data at the beginning of a research project as they often reveal issues which are of great concern to the target population, but may not have been brought to the attention of policymakers and service providers.

Each group discussion was tape-recorded and lasted an hour and a half. A free-flowing discussion guide was used which covered a range of topics related to the research objectives. However, the flexibility of the focus group format enabled participants to raise related issues which were of particular concern to them. For example, financial issues were a priority for many members of lower socioeconomic groups. Thus, personal finances and money worries in older age were discussed at length among the participants in several focus groups.

During Stage 1 of the study, 142 men and women aged 55 years and older took part in seventeen focus group discussions. Ten focus groups involving 85 men and women were held in three geographical areas of England that is, the North, the South and the Midlands. Twenty-four men and 24 women from the Bangladeshi, Pakistani and Indian communities living in a town in southern England took part in six focus groups. In addition, one focus group was conducted involving nine men and women from the Afro-Caribbean community in a town in southern England.

Two groups were solely composed of participants from socio-economic groups A, B and C1. The remaining fifteen groups involved men and women from socioeconomic groups C1/C2, D and E. Apart from one focus group where all the participants lived in residential homes, the remaining participants lived in the community in a variety of different types of accommodation. For the higher socioeconomic groups, this generally meant privately owned accommodation; participants from lower socioeconomic groups lived in private or local authority rented accommodation, or were owner occupiers.

Pakistani, Bangladeshi and Indian focus groups

The majority of participants from the Bangladeshi, Pakistani and Indian communities lived in an extended family network. Participants in the six focus group discussions were selected by means of community networking. Each group consisted of eight people and the only criterion for selection was that each participant should be aged 55 years or older; there was no upper age limit. In addition, care was taken to ensure that the sample included:

- women who had been in paid employment and women who had not
- individuals with differing levels of fluency in English
- literate and non-literate individuals.

The majority of the men were married and two had been widowed. The majority of the women were married; six had been widowed and one was divorced. The marital status of the men and women who participated in the focus groups reflected that of the wider population aged 55 years and older.

Afro-Caribbean focus group

Five women and four men took part in this focus group, all of whom were born in Barbados or Jamaica. All the women and one of the men were over 70 years of age, while the remaining three men were aged between 60 and 65. Two of the participants lived with their spouses, the remainder lived alone; one of the men was a recent widow.

Stage 2: In-depth interviews

The findings of the focus group discussions guided the development of the interview schedule used in the second stage of the study. Semi-structured interviews were used to examine the issues raised in focus groups in more depth. Interviewees were able to speak at length about their life experiences and health issues, and were able to raise topics which were of particular concern to them. Interviews, which were tape-recorded, were carried out in the homes of the participants and lasted between 1 and 2 hours.

In Stage 2 of the study, 90 men and women aged 55 years and older took part in in-depth interviews. Sixty men and women selected at random from the general population took part in interviews in rural and urban locations in three geographical areas of England, that is the North, the South and the Midlands. Twenty-four interviews took place with men and women from the Bangladeshi, Pakistani and Indian communities in a town in southern England. In addition, 6 Afro-Caribbean men and women living in an inner city London borough took part in interviews.

Sample

Interviewees were selected at random; however, care was taken to ensure that the sample included the following:
- a gender balance reflecting that of the wider population aged 55 and over
- individuals who were housebound
- men and women who lived alone
- individuals who were living on state benefits
- men and women who were suffering from chronic illness
- individuals living in sheltered, warden-assisted and residential accommodation.

Among the general sample, two-thirds of the interviewees were living alone; between weekly visits to a day centre, several interviewees routinely had no social contacts other than with voluntary or paid carers. The majority of the interviewees had received an elementary education and had left school before the age of 15 without any qualifications, although some participants had acquired professional or academic qualifications later. All the male interviewees and the majority of the female interviewees had retired from work. Six of the male interviewees had been professionals, managers or had run their own manufacturing businesses; one of the female interviewees was running her own wholesale business. The majority of the remaining interviewees had been skilled or semi-skilled workers, for example miners, factory workers, shop assistants and care workers.

Interviews with Pakistani and Bangladeshi respondents were carried out in Urdu and annotated verbatim in English. Interviews with Indian respondents were carried out and annotated in Hindi and later translated verbatim into English. Participants were selected at random through community networking and care was taken to ensure that the sample included the following:

- women who were, or had been, in paid employment outside the home
- individuals with differing levels of education
- widowed men and women who were living with one of their children
- at least one person who was living alone.

Among the Afro-Caribbean sample, all the interviewees were or had been in manual or unskilled occupations; two interviewees were still working. One male interviewee was a qualified primary school teacher, but had worked as a bus conductor; the remaining interviewees had no formal educational qualifications. Two interviewees were owner-occupiers and the remaining interviewees lived in local authority or housing association accommodation. All the female interviewees were single; one woman lived with her son and one woman lived with her sister. One man was divorced and lived alone; two men were married and lived with their partners.

Structure of the report

The findings of the study are presented in two parts; in Part 1, we examine the health beliefs of those who took part in the study, and discuss the wide range of socioeconomic, environmental and cultural factors which can affect older people's health. In Part 2, we investigate the extent to which older men and women practise health-promoting behaviours.

Part 1: Older people's health beliefs

In Chapter 1, we look at the ways in which participants conceptualised 'good' and 'poor' health, and examine how older people's definitions vary from those of younger people and differ according to age, ethnicity and gender. In Chapter 2, we investigate the factors which participants believed could affect the health of older people, including structural and cultural factors, the local and social environment, life events and personal circumstances, and personal behaviour. In Chapter 3, we move on to investigate participants' beliefs about the amount of control they have over their health.

Part 2: Older people's health-promoting behaviour

Chapter 4 examines participants' definitions of 'healthy behaviour', and the importance they attach to having a 'healthy lifestyle'. Chapter 5 seeks to identify the sources from which older people obtain information about health-related matters. In Chapter 6, we consider the factors which might deter older people from practising health-promoting behaviour. In conclusion, Chapter 7 discusses the findings and implications of the study and suggests ways in which organisations and health providers might approach health promotion for older people in the future.

Part 1

Older people's health beliefs

Part 1 of this report investigates older people's beliefs about health, focusing on three central issues: the meaning and consequences of 'good' and 'ill' health, factors which affect health in later life, and the extent to which older people feel that they have control over their health.

1 Conceptualising 'health'

This chapter explores the way in which the older people who took part in the study sought to define the concept of 'health'. In the majority of cases, perceptions of health and illness were influenced by the belief that although health and mobility problems are not inevitable in older age, they are certainly more common. Indeed, participants had a variety of ailments which they and their doctors attributed to older age such as late-onset diabetes, cataracts, osteoporosis, rheumatoid arthritis and Parkinson's disease. Many participants also reported that the process of ageing seemed to have had an effect on both their mental and physical capabilities, with the result that they were more prone to memory lapses and to minor ailments and accidents. The following comments were made about these issues:

You're bound to have some health problems unless you keep yourself very, very fit. Age catches up with you. You just have to keep going as long as you can.

Man, 57: General interviews, urban South

When you get to 60, you are past it. Certain things are never going to be the same again . . . Like, sometimes you can't get about as fast as you want to. Sometimes you can't remember things . . . You tend to get more colds. You tend to get flu a bit longer . . . Your eyesight goes, you can't see as well . . .

Woman: 55–64 focus group, urban South

Most times when I'm not feeling right I say it is old age. Old age causes most of the ills. Old age causes sickness. I put it down to that. I put everything down to old age.

Man, 79: Afro-Caribbean interviewee

In general, participants based their comments about health on personal experience and on comparisons between themselves and other people of the same age. A large number of people pointed out that it is impossible to define 'good' health and 'poor' health unless both have been experienced, for example:

I've always been used to having my health and then when I got ill, well, it makes you more aware of good health, what it means to you.

Man, 56: General interviews, rural North

You don't really think about health till you lose it.

Man, 68: General interviews, urban South

Definitions of health tended to focus on function, that is, what each participant's state of health allowed him or her to do, and on subjective feelings of 'wellness' and 'illness'. Blaxter (1990; 1995) and Calnan (1987) report similar findings among adults of all ages. However, Blaxter (1990; 1995) found that older people tend to view health in a more 'holistic' way than younger people and are more likely to include social factors, such as being able to go out and to mix with other people, in their definitions of 'good' and 'ill' health. In the present study, a large number of participants perceived health as a combination of physical, psychological and social factors, and felt that suffering problems in any of these areas could have a negative effect on feelings of wellness and ability to function. In seeking to define the importance of good health in later life, many participants cited the maxim that physical, mental and spiritual wellbeing is more important than material wealth:

To me, your health is the most important thing in one's life . . . and people seem to let it go by the wayside and I mean, to be honest, to be healthy is the ground roots of everything you can achieve or do in life.

Man: Afro-Caribbean focus group

It's [good health] *better than riches. It's the best thing in the world. You're more cheerful, you see things more cheerfully. You want to do things.*

Woman, 81: General interviews, rural Midlands

Yes, if you've got that [good health] *you've got everything you need. Money don't mean a thing. You might as well not be here without it.*

Man, 89: General interviews, urban Midlands

Good health is the most important thing in this life, after faith.

Man, 58: Indian interviewee

A rather more complex holistic approach to defining health was common to most of the South Asian participants, and was closely linked to Sikh, Muslim and Hindu religious beliefs. The majority of Indian, Bangladeshi and Pakistani participants viewed 'good' health as the product of a symbiotic relationship between the physical, psychological, spiritual and social aspects of their lives, and believed that lack of harmony between any of these areas could lead to 'ill' health. South Asian participants made the following comments about this issue:

I get along with everyone. I have lots of close friends who I have contact with regularly. If I am good to others then God will be good to me and bless me with good health and a long life. I love meeting new people. This gives me a sense of feeling young and vibrant. It also gives me a sense of belonging, when I know I have many friends and relatives. This makes me feel healthy. It gives me the desire to live.

Man, 74: Indian interviewee

That your body is in tune with your soul and that there is no conflict. You know, like the feeling of being on a crowded bus but still feeling as if you are alone.

Woman: Indian focus group

Good health of body and mind are important. When you are physically ill, this can most of the time be cured with medication, but if you are mentally ill then I don't think really that there is anything that can cure that illness. So, good health all over is important for life to be fulfilling.

Man, 58: Pakistani interviewee

In general, however, participants felt that 'health' is a difficult concept to define because it is an attribute that varies from day to day. The 'salutogenic' approach to assessing health described by Antonovsky (1984) suggests that rather than thinking in terms of being either 'well' or 'unwell', it is more useful to conceptualise health as a continuum running from 'health-ease' to 'dis-ease'; the individual may place him or herself at a different point on the continuum at different times (Sidell, 1995). This point was made by several participants in the present study, for example:

I feel pretty well. I have on/off periods. I have days when I don't want to do anything at all. It's not a feeling of mental lowness, it's physical weakness. There's no pain or anything.

Man, 67 (with Parkinson's disease): General interviews, rural South

When you have good health, you want to do things. On the days that I'm feeling well, I want my daughter-in-law to take me to the bazaar. Otherwise, I just stay at home and pray.

Woman, 87: Indian interviewee

Very few of the older people who took part in the study defined 'good' health and wellbeing as the absence of disease. Indeed, some participants felt that it is possible to have a life-threatening medical condition yet to feel 'healthy' and reasonably contented with life. For example, this woman had breast cancer but, in the long term, her medical condition had not affected her ability to look after herself and her home, and she was able to enjoy a full and active social life:

I'm lucky. I'm quite healthy. I've just had my check-up at the hospital and they've called me in for another look. That's a bit of a worry, but I feel OK in myself. I have to take a lot of tablets but everything's normal apart from that.

Woman, 72: General interviews, rural South

The majority of participants shared this woman's view that the key indicators of 'good' health are having the ability, energy and self-motivation to carry out the daily necessities of life unaided, such as washing and dressing oneself, going to work, doing the household chores and socialising. The self-esteem generated by being 'healthy', independent and self-sufficient also enhanced participants' feelings of emotional wellbeing. The following comments were made about these issues:

Not being able to do for yourself. When you get up in the morning and you get that feeling that you cannot do that anymore, to me that is bad health.

Woman: Afro-Caribbean focus group

For me, doing things on my own, not asking anyone for help, and knowing that you are capable of everything, is health. If you have this then you know that you are well

Man, 72: Indian interviewee

Another factor which was associated with feeling 'healthy' in later life was the absence of severe physical pain. Aches and pains resulting from past injuries or deteriorating joints were seen as an inevitable consequence of the physiological process of ageing. If the sufferer could still carry out routine daily tasks, non-painful ailments and stiffness in the joints were not viewed as 'poor' health, for example:

I had an operation on both my knees because when I was in the British Army I was an all-round sportsman and the surgeon said to me what I have done to my knees, they are all mashed up. An operation on both of them made them worse. That's why I am walking with a stick now. But apart from the knees and the diabetes, I'm OK, fairly all right. I mean, I can't work because of blood pressure and all that, but I'm OK. I hold my own for my age. Man: Afro-Caribbean focus group

With my age and my illness, I would say I am fairly well. I can still get around. I can still think. I'm involved with the various organisations that I used to be involved with before, but not as active as before. So, I'm fairly well, and my voice is still very strong, which I'm proud of. Man: Afro-Caribbean focus group

However, people experiencing the intractable pain of chronic debilitating conditions such as rheumatoid arthritis were more likely to describe their health as 'poor' than participants with life-threatening ailments whose pain was well managed. Regardless of their levels of perceived and received support, participants with severe chronic pain generally felt that they lacked all the criteria of 'good' health, that is, the ability, energy and self-motivation to carry out the necessities of daily life. Indeed, the majority of the participants who described their health as 'poor' were from the 75+ age group and were experiencing intractable pain, or had other debilitating symptoms such as breathlessness; most were housebound, and some reported that they often had suicidal thoughts:

My health's not worth having. I can hardly talk. I'm out of breath all the time. I can't walk. I can't go out. I can't exert myself at all.

Woman, 76 (with emphysema): General interviews, urban North

It's very poor. It's the pain, it's constant. I can't get any relief from it. I mean, it affects how I feel all the time. What can I do? Life's not worth living.

Woman, 89 (with rheumatoid arthritis): General interviews, urban Midlands

Blaxter (1990; 1995) found that older people viewed being fit enough to help and support other people as a sign of 'good' health. During discussion groups with older people, Grundy (1994) was 'struck by how many of the oldest respondents in good physical and mental shape had outgoing personalities and a strong commitment to making other people's lives brighter and better' (p. 25). In the present study, many participants felt that being able to take an active role in the family and the community is an indicator of 'good' health. For example, a large number of white and Afro-Caribbean men and women, and South Asian men, were involved in family and community activities:

I organise the outings. I collect fish and chips for everyone on a Friday. I call the bingo, help with the barbecues in the summer. It got a bit too much for me. I'm not on the committee any more. I get tired, but I do what I can. I can still join in.

Man, 84: General interviews, urban South

I'm very involved in the church, and I do a lot of work for charity. We help Christians in the Sudan. And I go to the exercise class every week.

Man, 89: General interviews, rural South

Oh yes, well, I'm kept active, I'm able to help others. Also my grandchildren. I have seven. Five of them I see daily and I accompany them to the park while their parents are at work and things like that.

Man, 70: Afro-Caribbean interviewee

I have three sons who all live down the road from me. They all go out to work and I take their children to school and pick them up. So, during the day, I am busy . . .

Man: Indian focus group

In contrast, none of the South Asian women who took part in the study mentioned being active in the community, although a few felt that they made a useful contribution to family life. For example, this woman cooked the evening meal for twenty members of her family every day:

It might seem strange, but if I know that any of my children have not eaten then I cannot be peaceful. My husband is very good. He helps me with the cooking and everything . . . My children apart from the one all live on the same road. Now, we

could eat on our own in our own houses, but what is the point? I get to spend time with my children, my grandchildren and also the rest of the family. This is what makes me feel young and alive.   Woman, 72: Pakistani interviewee

It was evident from both focus groups and interviews that older South Asian women's lives tend to centre on their homes. Although the woman in the previous extract was still living in her own home, it is more usual among Indian, Pakistani and Bangladeshi families for elderly parents, especially if they are widowed, to live with one of their sons whose wife is expected to care for them as well as her own family. South Asian community leaders and health service providers who contributed background information to the study pointed out that changes have taken place in South Asian family life in recent years. Thus, in the UK and in the Indian subcontinent, increasing numbers of older men and women are now living alone. However, the majority of the people who took part in the study lived, or expected to live, with one of their sons and his family, either in their own home or in his; some of the younger participants were caring for their parents or parents-in-law. This caused increased stress levels for participants who were daughters-in-law of the family and for the older men and women who were being cared for, some of whom felt that they no longer had opportunities in the home to keep active or to make themselves useful. Furthermore, although this was not an issue in the present study, informants point out that the relationship between mother-in-law and daughter-in-law is often poor or confrontational (Choudry, 1996).

The effect of South Asian cultural traditions on health and well-being was a key area of discussion for participants in both focus groups and interviews, and is discussed in more detail in Chapter 2. However, this participant's comments suggest that although older South Asian women also associate good health with remaining active and having a useful role, they may be obliged to become dependent on others:

I just pray that I die before my husband because for a woman after her husband has gone it is very difficult to live. She becomes dependent on others around her. She cannot live in her own home and she has no say, I think, in her life.
                                        Woman, 59: Pakistani interviewee

2   Factors which affect health in older age

This chapter examines a number of factors which can affect the experience of health in older age, focusing on the links between structural and cultural factors, life events, personal circumstances, and behaviour.

1. Structural and cultural factors

In this section, we examine variations in the life and health expectancy of older people, and the way in which ageist perceptions of the characteristics of older people affect their social position. In addition, we examine cultural variations in beliefs about health in later life.

Since the turn of the century, the proportion of older people in the UK population has been rising steadily, and is projected to rise still further. This is due to a number of factors including falling birth and death rates, and increasing life expectancy as a result of a higher standard of living and increased welfare and medical services. Whereas life expectancy at birth in 1901 was 45.5 years for men and 49 years for women, average life expectancy for a child born in the 1990s is 74.4 years for men and 79.7 years for women (OPCS, 1996). Furthermore, the longer an individual lives, the more his or her overall life expectancy increases. Thus, a man who reaches his sixtieth birthday in the 1990s can expect to live, on average, for a further 22.6 years; if that same man lives to celebrate his eightieth birthday, his life expectancy will increase to over 88 years. Men and women aged 85 years and older now comprise 1.8 per cent of the British population; by the year 2011, people aged over 65 years are expected to comprise 17 per cent of the population (OPCS, 1996, cited in Ginn, Arber and Cooper, 1997).

Despite their growing numerical strength, however, older people continue to be perceived as a 'minority' in the sense that, as a social group, their characteristics, needs and attitudes are assumed to be significantly different from those of the rest of the population. For example, older age is associated with an increased risk of physical and mental health problems, and with disability, dependency and death. However, research indicates that older people's health experiences are as varied as those of any other age group (Ginn, Arber and Cooper, 1997). The human life span is 115 years (Grimley Evans, 1994) and although few individuals reach this age, many people remain active and in good physical and mental health well into their eighth or ninth decades; for example, only 7 per cent of people between 65 and 80 suffer from dementia, and 95 per cent of people aged 65 and over live in their own homes (Giddens, 1997). Yet, older people continue to be stereotyped as dependent, senile and institutionalised, and as a burden on their families and the welfare state.

'Ageism', that is, stereotyping people on the grounds of age, contributes to age stratification and structured dependency throughout the industrialised world. As a result of this, both the young and the old are denied status and responsibility. For example, younger people are assumed to be careless and unreliable, and older people are assumed to lack stamina and mental agility; furthermore, the oldest members of society are assumed to be as incapable of looking after themselves as the youngest. With the exception of a few 'elder statesmen', older people have a low status throughout the developed world. The devaluation of older people results largely from the process of industrialisation and the development of the waged economy. Based on the assumption that the onset of old age signals the imminence of senility, disablement and death, older individuals are expected to disengage from social life, that is, to relinquish their social roles and their position in the workforce in favour of younger people. In comparison, status and value tend to increase with age in non-industrialised societies. In such societies, older members of the community work for as long as they are able; they are assumed to have greater wisdom by virtue of their life experience, and are asked for advice when major decisions have to be taken. In industrialised societies, however, older people's knowledge and skills are often seen as out of date and irrelevant, particularly in the modern workplace. Furthermore, older people are perceived as inflexible and unable to cope with the fast pace of social and technological change.

Although women have a longer life expectancy and predominate in older age groups, they tend to have even less social status than older men. During most of the twentieth century, women in industrialised societies have been confined to the home or concentrated in low-paid, part-time work. Thus, apart from raising the next generation of workers and taking the place of male workers during wartime, retired older women are considered to have made only a modest contribution to the economy of industrialised societies. Because older women's working lives tend to have been fragmented as a result of staying at home to care for children or other members of the family, many have not had the opportunity to save or contribute to a pension fund. In consequence, not only are older women more likely than men to be living alone, but they are more likely to be living on low incomes. Older women from minority ethnic groups are at even greater risk of poverty since, even if they were in continuous full-time employment through-out their working lives, they are more likely to have been in the lowest paid occupations such as domestic and unskilled manual work.

In general, however, fewer older people now live in poverty in the UK than was the case at the beginning of the century, when the poor could expect to end their lives in the workhouse. Nevertheless, despite state and employment pensions and state benefits, large numbers of older men and women live on incomes that are lower than they received before retirement and are lower than the national average. Furthermore, Walker and Maltby (1997) point out that the gap between the wealthiest and the poorest older people is steadily increasing so that the UK now has one of the highest poverty rates among older people in Europe. Research indicates that health status in older age is closely linked to previous occupational class and, in the case of older women, to the occupational class of their husbands. Older people who worked in manual occupations are more likely to suffer chronic and disabling medical conditions in retirement than those in professional occupations (Ginn, Arber and Cooper, 1997). Because income in older age is influenced by income before retirement, older people in low-paid occupations, and those who experienced long periods of unemployment, may well live in poorer quality housing in run-down areas, they may have no access to private transport, and they may not be able to afford to heat their homes adequately or to buy good quality food.

Ginn, Arber and Cooper (1997) argue that 'occupational class extends its influence on health beyond the working life, both directly and through its effect on the standard of living in later life' (p. 17). Thus, participants in the present study were selected to represent a wide range of socioeconomic circumstances, and the sample included men and women who were still in work, people who had been unemployed for most of their working lives, and people who had retired from occupations as diverse as shop work, mining and the judiciary. Participants' personal circumstances were equally diverse. Some participants lived on extremely low incomes in tower blocks in deprived inner-city areas; others lived in run-down bungalows in isolated rural hamlets or in comfortable detached houses in tree-lined suburban avenues. However, for a number of participants, their personal circumstances were influenced by their ethnicity, that is, their racial and cultural origins. With the exception of migration, the life experiences and socioeconomic circumstances of Afro-Caribbean participants were broadly similar to those of older men and women sampled from the general population. However, there were a number of differences in the life experiences of South Asian participants. In the UK, there has been only limited and small-scale research into the health of older members of minority ethnic groups, largely because they are small in number; Arber and Ginn (1991) found that, in the 1980s, retired men and women from minority ethnic groups comprised only 1 per cent of the UK population, although they point out that this proportion is likely to rise as minority ethnic populations age. Researchers argue that the relationship between ethnicity and health in later life is an extremely complex issue which requires more extensive research. In the present study, factors such as the experience of migration and cultural traditions regarding the living arrangements of older people in the South Asian community appeared to be linked to the health experiences of female participants in particular. These and other structural and cultural factors which affect the health and wellbeing of older people are explored in the following sections of this chapter.

Ageism

The findings of the present study indicate that the views of many of the participants were influenced by ageist perceptions and attitudes. For example, there was a widespread expectation that increasing age would lead to senility, disablement, dependency and, possibly, the need for residential care:

The biggest dread of my life, and always will be, is having to go into a home. It's the biggest dread of my life, and I will do anything to avoid it.

Man: 75+ focus group, urban Midlands

I don't want to end up in one of them. I want to stay in my own home and do what I want. Woman: 75+ focus group, urban North

I'm always worried in case I have to go into a home. You hear such terrible stories about old people being beaten and abused. And who's going to look after me when I get older? It's a big worry having no family.

Man, 85: General interviews, urban North

However, some participants were aware that internalised ageism, combined with the ageist attitudes of younger people, can lead fit and able older people into a state of dependency. In general, these participants believed that dependency results not only in physical inactivity, which can have negative consequences for general health, but also in loss of self-confidence and self-esteem which can have a negative impact on emotional wellbeing. Research indicates that resisting ageist stereotypes leads to better health for older people; for example, Grimley Evans (1994) suggests that 'those people who insist on staying in control of their own lives, the wilful and cantankerous, live longer than the more compliant "sweet old folk"' (p. 19). Many of the participants were of the same opinion, and their views were shared by the majority of the community leaders and health service providers who contributed background information for the study. Participants made the following comments about this issue:

I've got friends younger than me who've given up. They have 'Meals on Wheels', home helps. They don't even do their own washing. You've got to keep control on your own life, not let other people take it over. They tell you to do daft things. They make people weaker, like my friend. This doctor says 'Don't go out in the kitchen making tea'. Now she thinks she shouldn't do anything for herself.

Woman, 75: General interviews, urban South

I know that some try to be dependent on others rather than trying to help themselves . . . they get a bit of trouble, feel sorry for yourself and let others do it for you, wherein if you make the effort to counteract that, you can overcome it.

Man, 70: Afro-Caribbean interviewee

With Mom [a friend living in sheltered accommodation], *although she can't hardly stand up, she would still rather be by that cooker turning over that piece of salt-fish the way she wants it than having cottage pie with mashed potatoes coming from downstairs.*

Man: Afro-Caribbean focus group

There were significant differences between the types of ageism experienced by South Asian participants and those from the white and Afro-Caribbean samples. Pakistani, Bangladeshi and Indian participants felt that in their communities people generally achieve higher status and responsibility as they grow older, especially men. Nevertheless, enhanced status can also result in older people becoming dependent because younger people are obliged to demonstrate the respect they have for older relatives by providing for all their material and personal needs.

South Asian community leaders and care workers who provided background information for the study suggested that some older people, especially women, insist upon receiving a high level of care because they devoted much of their youth to caring for older relatives. A few of the younger women who took part in the study had been obliged to give up their careers and their lives outside the home in order to care for parents-in-law who, in some cases, were well able to look after themselves. One of the male participants made the following comments about this issue:

I like to do everything myself. My wife wants me to keep asking my daughter-in-law for things, even like a glass of water. She says it is her duty to take care of us. But for me, if I can do things myself I know I'm healthy.

Man: Bangladeshi focus group

However, as noted in Chapter 1, many of the South Asian women who took part in the study did not perceive older age as 'pay-back time', but as a time when they were obliged by cultural tradition to be inactive while their daughters-in-law appropriated all their domestic responsibilities. Participants made the following comments about the detrimental effects that this arrangement had on their health and wellbeing:

*Caring for my mother-in-law, it has left me feeling drained. I also took early retirement because of her and I miss my work.*Woman, 56: Indian interviewee

I think once my husband died, my life changed completely. I was no longer able to run my own home. Sometimes I've lived with one son, sometimes with the other. My children have been very good, but it is still not like living in your own home.
Woman, 78: Bangladeshi interviewee

For some participants, these age-related changes in the pattern of their lives brought about feelings of loneliness, worthlessness and apathy. Indeed, several of the South Asian women from the older age groups had disengaged from social life to such an extent that they felt that their lives no longer had any purpose other than to make spiritual preparations for death:

I'm prepared to move on to a better life, I think. This material life no longer has a purpose for me. I think these last days of life are always the most difficult.
Woman, 75: Indian interviewee

I remember God now all the time. There are times when I do not get off my prayer mat and sit on it all day. This is really all that will benefit me in my life after death. All these worldly things will be left behind. Woman: Pakistani focus group

This was a key area of discussion among the female participants, several of whom felt that South Asian women are prone to 'let themselves go' in later life largely, they felt, in response to cultural expectations about how older women should behave. Participants made the following comments about this issue:

There are some women who will not accept that they are old and will dress in bright clothes and do a lot of fashion, but they do not realise that people talk about them behind their backs, and they say things like 'She wants to stay young . . .'
Woman: Bangladeshi focus group

Often our women . . . feel that it is better for them not to take care of themselves. They think this is a good thing to do once they are old, you know, not paying attention to yourself. This kind of behaviour makes you feel even older than you are.
Woman, 58: Bangladeshi interviewee

As you get older, you are treated differently in our culture. For example, whenever there is a decision to be made I am always asked first. The older people in our

community are treated with respect. But along with this respect, society expects you to stop living. If I wear good clothes, I am criticised for not acting my age. I am expected to wear white clothes. Most of the old women do anyway but you get fed up, do you know what I mean? My husband is still alive. I like to dress up for him, but at the risk of being made fun of. What can you do? You have to start acting like an old woman even if you do not want to. We live in a complex society.

Woman: Pakistani focus group, urban South

Many older South Asian men also believed that cultural traditions which result in inactivity and dependency can have a negative impact on health and wellbeing in later life, for example:

There was immense pressure from the family to marry again, but I couldn't do that. I loved my wife, I wanted to keep her memories alive. Then my eldest son was married and I now have a wonderful daughter-in-law at home. My relatives said to me 'Now you can stop doing all the housework. You have a daughter-in-law to take care of you'. But I don't believe in all that. If I was to sit down and expect her to wait on me, then I would be doing myself harm.

Man, 78: Bangladeshi interviewee

My children and my daughter-in-law are very good. They all take care of me, but it is not the same. I always depended on my wife for everything and for me that was quite normal. Having to ask my children for something is not right, I don't feel the same. Man, 78: Pakistani interviewee

Many participants felt that health problems in older age were caused by the stress embedded in South Asian family and community life, for example:

Well, the Asian way of life is very stressful. You are always expected to cope with everything and as you get older you are naturally expected to cope with other people's problems as well as your own. It just gets really hard sometimes.

Man, 67: Pakistani interviewee

Not being well, either that you do not eat properly, you have worries about your children, especially your daughters, about their future . . .

Woman, 67: Pakistani interviewee

With our men there are a lot of family problems. Because of their honour and shame they try and pretend that nothing is happening. They will not seek advice from anywhere but instead bear the burden of their troubles on their own. For our people it is better to go hungry, but respect within the community is something that is the most important thing to so many men.

Man, 76: Bangladeshi interviewee

Financial circumstances

Nevertheless, participants felt that certain features of South Asian family life can help to enhance health and feelings of wellbeing. For example, as community leaders and health service providers pointed out, despite changing patterns of family life fewer older South Asian people live solely on state pensions and benefits than might be the case among the general population. Indeed, financial issues were not mentioned by any of the South Asian participants, although this may have been due, in part, to the same reluctance to discuss personal finances that was evident among some of the white and Afro-Caribbean participants.

Other participants, however, were far less reticent about discussing money. For example, lack of financial resources occupied much of the discussion in focus groups involving members of the general population in London and in the rural South. During preliminary research for the study, a large number of care providers felt that having an income just above the level at which they were eligible for state benefits was the cause of serious money worries for many of their clients. It was pointed out that being in receipt of a employer's pension of less than a pound a week could deprive a client of financial and welfare benefits worth hundreds of pounds a year. Furthermore, it was felt that dealing with bills and financial 'paperwork' could be an additional source of worry, especially for the very old. One of the participants, who works as a home carer, discussed this issue in her interview:

Some of the old people I work with can get a bill and it may be high because of a mistake, and they worry about how they are going to pay the bill. They don't know how to deal with the mistake.   Woman, 59: Afro-Caribbean interviewee

These observations were endorsed by the comments of the older people who took part in the study, some of whom, especially in the lower socioeconomic groups, were so worried about getting into debt that they deprived themselves of adequate food, heating and medical treatment:

The thing is if you have got money then you can eat decently. I can't afford three meals a day, which I should have.

Woman: 55–64 focus group, London

I put off having my eyes tested because I know I can't afford a new prescription for my lenses. I know my eyes are getting worse, but there's nothing I can do about it.

Woman: 65–74 focus group, rural South

We work all the days of our life . . . and they can't even give us the money to buy

food. Black and white are in this situation. You either heat the house or eat, you can't do both.   Woman, 62: Afro-Caribbean interviewee

I speak to some people and all they talk about is money, money and if you are thinking about only money . . . it must mash you up, it worry you so much.   Woman, 79: Afro-Caribbean interviewee

However, even where participants were reluctant to discuss their personal circumstances, many of the issues they raised suggested that there were financial constraints upon them which impinged upon their general health and wellbeing. For example, a large number of participants clearly felt that their quality of life was adversely affected by being unable to afford transport. Participants felt that it was extremely important for health and wellbeing to 'get out of the house' on a regular basis:

Imagine being shut up indoors all day. I would go crazy.   Woman: 75+ focus group, urban South

Nevertheless, some participants mentioned that they never had holidays or trips away from home. Several participants from rural areas who were fit and able to lead a full and active social life were prevented from doing so because bus services were inadequate and they could not afford to run a car. Less able participants in rural areas reported that they often put off going to the doctor, optician and chiropodist not only because of the cost of the treatment but also because of the cost of transport; for example, a woman living in the rural South reported paying over £12.00 in taxi fares for a round trip to her GP's surgery. Furthermore, the majority of participants in both rural and urban settings were afraid to go out at night on foot; thus, unless they could afford their own vehicle, the cost of taxis prevented them from going to social events, concerts or the theatre in the evening, except on rare occasions. Participants made the following comments about the way in which being unable to afford transport affects their wellbeing and quality of life:

. . . you stay in the same place every single day of your life, what have you got to look forward to? You don't live, you exist . . . I have nothing to look forward to . . . everything is on the same level. There are no plateaux, how can you say that is life?   Woman: 55–64 focus group, London

I haven't been to one in years [an optician]. My eyes are bad now, it's getting there's the problem. I don't like to keep bothering the neighbours, they take me to the doctor's and shopping.   Man (diabetic), 89: General interviews, rural Midlands

However, in some rural areas there were thriving voluntary driver organisations in operation which, as long as older people were aware of them, could provide free or modestly priced door-to-door transport to hospital appointments, social events or to visit friends. Older people living in inner cities generally felt that, during daylight hours at least, they were well served by public transport. All had bus passes allowing them to travel free or for reduced fares; many had a choice of several nearby routes, and buses were frequent. Apart from those living in isolated rural areas, the most disadvantaged participants in terms of transport were those who lived on outer-city estates with few local amenities, for example:

It's a cultural desert. There's no nothing. No community centre, no shops. They're miles away and you daren't walk anywhere round here. There's no cinema. And no church, the nearest one's in town. You have to go on the bus, and there's hardly any of them. It's as bad as living in the countryside.

Woman, 62: General interviews, urban Midlands

Participants who lived in their own homes also mentioned the worry of maintaining their properties, for example, decorating and making repairs. Many people received help from family and friends. However, a few participants were unable to carry out their own decorating or to look after their gardens but could not afford to pay someone to do these tasks for them. Most were distressed by their overgrown gardens and the deteriorating appearance of their homes, and were worried that the neglect would cause structural damage and damp. In comparison, people who lived in sheltered accommodation and in residential care were relieved of these anxieties, for example:

I was worried when they said I had to go into a home. I was frightened, but I've settled down now, really quickly. Everything's taken care of, I don't have to worry about money. It's like being in a big family.

Woman, 72: General interviews, urban North

Personal safety and security

As a result of media publicity about such incidents, the majority of participants felt that they were more vulnerable to crime, sudden illness and accidents now that they were older. Thus, enhanced personal safety was frequently cited as an additional advantage to living in sheltered, residential and warden-assisted accommodation in later life, although a number of people reported that determined thieves can find a way into even the most secure blocks. For example, this man lived in a warden-assisted council-owned tower block which had been specially adapted for occupation by people with mobility problems:

We've had drug addicts, muggings. Here. In this block. They broke down the security door to get in the last time. Man, 84: General interviews, urban South

Likewise, people living on the ground floor in both private and council-owned sheltered accommodation felt that they were more vulnerable to burglary and attack than people living on the first floor and above.

Nevertheless, participants felt safer, especially at night, as a result of knowing that there was a warden on the premises to help them in an emergency. There was a widespread fear among participants that they might collapse or die, and that no one would find them for days. Consequently, being regularly contacted by a warden, relative or neighbour gave people additional peace of mind. Many participants who lived alone in their own houses subscribed to private or local authority 'alarm call' schemes whereby they wore a communication device around their necks which they could use to summon help via the telephone in an emergency.

The local environment

In general, feelings of good health and wellbeing were associated with living in a well-maintained and well-equipped home in a quiet, clean environment. Participants living in purpose-built sheltered accommodation tended to be particularly happy with their environment; even where flats were located in inner-city settings, they generally had gardens which provided a pleasant outlook and enabled residents to sit outside in the summer. Nevertheless, a small number of people who lived in run-down terraced houses and tower-block flats in inner-city areas also felt happy with their environment. This was largely because they had lived there for many years, knew all their neighbours and had a wide range of amenities nearby. In general, participants felt safer and happier if they were part of a close-knit, supportive community, for example:

I just lost my wife, what, three months ago, and it's traumatic. But fortunately for me I have been supported greatly by the members of the church . . . Apart from that, my neighbours as well. I have lived in a cul-de-sac for the past thirty-eight years and all my children grew up with young couples that moved in the same time as me, and I am wellknown in that area, and well thought of by quite a number of the neighbours, and they have supported me greatly . . . I have been fortunate enough to live in a neighbourhood where I could get quite a bit of help.

Man: Afro-Caribbean focus group

In general, the participants who were most satisfied with their environment were those living in rural areas, and those living in inner-city areas in the Midlands and South. For example, participants living in the urban South, close to the sea, made the following comments:

It's [a mobile home] *a bit cold in winter, but look at that. People'd pay a fortune for a place in that marina and not have a better view. The boats, the weather, lot of water when the tide's in. Wonderful.*
Man (recent amputee), 68: General interviews, urban South

It's nice living here, by the sea. They do such lovely things with the gardens. I know it's for the holidaymakers, but the flowers, the trees. And these blocks. They're all beautifully landscaped. The council do it. You don't get that in some places.
Man, 88: General interviews, urban South

Several participants living in the urban North were less happy with their environment and felt that they were more likely to be victimised by crime, and that they were being exposed to too much industrial and traffic pollution, for example:

I feel healthier now I've moved away from the city a bit. It's not so smoky.
Woman, 66: General interviews, urban North

Participants who were least happy with their environment tended to live on outer-city housing estates, and many of them felt that their environment had a detrimental effect on their health and wellbeing. Participants believed that they were at constant risk of crimes such as mugging and vandalism, and that they were suffering 'noise pollution' as a result of children and young people gathering outside their homes to play football or take drugs. A small number of people had bought their homes which had since become difficult to sell because of their location; others had been on council waiting-lists for a move for many years. Some felt so desperate to leave their present accommodation that they often had suicidal thoughts.

The social environment

Although all the people who lived on outer-city estates were liable to be disadvantaged by their poor environment, many younger people left the area each day to go to school or to work or to visit friends elsewhere. However, older people felt themselves to be trapped by lack of money and transport, and this woman's comments represent the views of many participants who lived on such estates:

People are afraid to leave their houses at night. Nothing gets done about the crime. It's down to apathy. I feel like I'm in a prison.

Woman, 62: General interviews, urban Midlands

Participants who lived in sheltered or residential accommodation generally felt that peace of mind and reduced financial outgoings outweighed the disadvantages of community living. Nevertheless, some of the men and women from the general population were uneasy about what they perceived as the 'ghettoisation' of older people. Several felt that it suits younger members of society to 'shunt' older people into their own communities where they can live and socialise almost exclusively with each other. Furthermore, some participants objected to perceptions of older people as a homogeneous group who prefer passive activities such as watching television, playing bingo and going on coach trips.

Participants acknowledged that wardens and organisations such as Age Concern provide a valuable service in terms of entertainment and welfare care. Indeed, male and female participants from all age groups belonged to groups for older people. However, many preferred to be involved in organising activities, preparing meals and acting as voluntary drivers for less able and active older people than themselves. Arber and Ginn (1995) argue that voluntary work, especially for older women, may be a 'bourgeois option, unavailable to those who have low incomes and poor health' (p. 8). In the present study, however, participants regarded 'voluntary work' as any type of assistance given to other people. Thus, regardless of income and state of health, many of the men and women who took part in the study were regularly visiting or going shopping for housebound neighbours, or cooking meals for other people.

This finding supports the argument by Jerrome (1986) that, in general, older people find voluntary work and socialising with friends and relatives preferable to taking part in 'old people's activities'. Several participants in the present study said that they made a point of refusing invitations to join in activities which they perceived as being 'specially for old people', preferring to remain at home or to make their own amusement. Nevertheless, the oldest and least physically able participants derived a great deal of enjoyment from activities organised for older people, for example:

I get out and about with Age Concern. I get two good meals. I play games, dominoes, bingo. I think it keeps my brain active.

Woman, 94: General interviews, rural Midlands

It's most important to see your friends and have company. I go to the day centre every Friday. A mini-bus picks me up. I like to go for the company. I look forward to it.
Man, 85: General interviews, urban Midlands

I just look forward to getting up and going into the community centre. Our community has managed to arrange to have drop-in sessions for people of my age. We all get together, have a cup of tea, and sit and chat. Then I go to the mosque for the prayers and generally keep myself busy.
Man: Pakistani focus group

Well, I would go into a decline if I hadn't got here [a day centre]. *I hate being shut in, so it's lovely to know you can get out.*
Woman: 75+ focus group, urban South

Some of the oldest participants found that they had little in common with the other users of older people's social clubs and day centres, but continued to go because it was an opportunity to get out of the house once or twice a week. The same complaint was made about the social life in nursing homes:

I had to go into a home after the fire. I didn't like it. There was no company. The only other man in there, all he cared about was horse racing.
Man, 89: General interviews, urban Midlands

I had to go in a home when my daughter went to New Zealand. The staff were nice but . . . They didn't lay on anything for you to do, most of them were too far gone.
Woman, 94: General interviews, urban Midlands

These comments were made by two of the oldest participants in the study, both of whom felt lonely and isolated largely because it seemed to them that they were far more mentally alert and interested in life than most of their contemporaries. Jerrome (1986) found that older people prefer to mix with people from all age groups, and it was certainly the case in the present study that a number of participants felt that they had more in common with people younger than themselves.

Social isolation

Loneliness was a key issue for discussion among the white and Afro-Caribbean participants, most of whom were living alone. Self-assessments of 'poor' health were closely associated with lack of perceived social support from family members, neighbours and friends. Conversely, self-assessment of 'good' health in the presence of chronic or life-threatening ailments was associated with the availability of social support which enabled older people to remain active within their communities. Participants generally felt less isolated if they lived in sheltered accommodation or in communities where they had regular contact with their neighbours, for example:

. . . it is important to have close friends and relatives to keep in close contact and keep in touch with them so if anything befalls you, apart from the doctors and the nurses or whoever, there is a close back-up. People that can take you to the hospital, can take you to the doctor's, can come up and have a word with you. So I've always kept in close contact with friends and neighbours as an alternative back-up in case anything happened to me that I couldn't cope with.

Man: Afro-Caribbean focus group

Nevertheless, all the participants who lived alone said that they felt lonely from time to time, especially in the evenings, and some had the television switched on during all their waking hours 'for the company'.

Some of the oldest participants, and many of those with mobility problems, felt themselves to be isolated largely by the attitudes of other people. There was a widespread belief, especially among those who took part in interviews, that younger people and their more able-bodied contemporaries 'could not be bothered' with them because they were frail and slow-moving. For example, this man felt that he had a poor quality of life because members of the surrounding community avoided personal contact with him, so that he had regular contact only with his home carer:

The next-door neighbours keep an eye on me, but they don't call in. They just ring up to see if I'm all right.   Man, 89: General interviews, urban Midlands

This younger woman also felt that she had a poor quality of life. She was retired from work and lived alone. A lack of financial resources meant that she had access to a social club only once a month and, apart from this, she had little social contact with anyone:

All I want to do is, tomorrow I don't want to wake up, that's all . . . What's the point? You just go through every day exactly the same.

Woman: 55–64 focus group, London

However, Grundy (1994) argues that although the number of people living alone in later life is steadily rising, this does not necessarily indicate a trend towards the wholesale neglect and abandonment of older people by younger members of society. She points out that in the majority of cases, older people live alone by choice because they want to, because they have the means to do so and because they prefer to be independent. Indeed, the health and care workers who provided background information for the present study felt that it is important for older people's self-esteem that they are treated as capable and able adults, and that unwanted help and attention are not forced on them, however frail they may be. The majority of the participants in the present study were determined to remain independent, and to do as much as possible for themselves.

A number of participants felt that a degree of loneliness was the 'price' they had to pay for maintaining their independence in their own homes. Nevertheless, knowing that practical help, emotional support and companionship were readily available if required contributed in great measure to feelings of general wellbeing. Participants made the following comments about the effect that lack of social contact and support can have on health and wellbeing:

When I'm on my own, I feel so miserable not having anyone to speak to.
Woman: 65–74 focus group, North

Recently my husband died so I do feel lonely, more than ever. So you need to be among people and, well, I don't know what it does to your health, but you certainly feel better in yourself. Woman: 55–64 focus group, London

Sometimes loneliness cause you to just sit there and think all kinds of stupidness, and sometimes it make you ill . . .
Woman, 62: Afro-Caribbean interviews, inner-city London

In a study which she and Ann Bowling carried out for the Joseph Rowntree Foundation, Grundy (1994) found that, among the general population, 'very few elderly people lack emotional and social ties' (p. 24). This was certainly the case in the present study; nearly all the participants had daily contact with family members, neighbours or care workers. Many fit and able participants felt that they benefited from being able to offer help and support to neighbours and younger members of the family by doing their shopping, baby-sitting and lending a sympathetic ear in times of trouble. Less able-bodied participants welcomed the practical help and emotional support that they received from neighbours and friends, for example:

I get a lot of help from my family. I was angry when they turned me down for the Attendance Allowance for my daughter. She's got a full-time job but she does all my washing, drives me to the bank, everything . . .
Man, 68: General interviews, urban South

The majority of participants were satisfied with the level of contact they had with neighbours and relatives. However, many men and women missed the quiet, undemanding companionship that they had enjoyed with a 'significant other', such as their spouse, a friend, a child, a parent or a sibling; that is, the type of relationship in which they could talk if they felt like it, or remain silent without causing offence. Some older or more infirm participants felt that, as they had become more housebound, they had lost control over their social lives. For example, one woman praised the system which operated in her sheltered accommodation whereby residents left their front doors ajar during the day if they wanted relatives, care workers or their neighbours to call in for a chat, and shut their doors if they wanted to be quiet and alone for a while. Indeed, several participants made the point that the need for companionship in later life varies considerably from day to day, and from person to person, for example:

I think it's a question of personality. Some people need more company than others.
Man, 86: General interviews, rural Midlands

The urge to go out and mix? Well, it depends how you feel on the day.
Man, 80: General interviews, rural South

Thus, when participants spoke of loneliness some made it clear that they did not necessarily mean the complete absence of social contact but the absence of the right kind of social contact, that is, social contact on their own terms, and with people with whom they had something in common other than family ties or old age. Others spoke of the value that they placed on friendship, because their friends were the people with whom they chose to socialise. However, several participants were aware that the range and quality of their social relationships, and their choice of companions, were steadily dwindling as they became older. Participants made the following comments about this issue:

Of course, I would like to live with my daughter, but daughters are things that you give away to others not keep yourself. Woman: Pakistani focus group

I'm still in touch with my mate from the Royals [Royal Marines]. *You know, they're sometimes better than your family, your mates. Not being ungrateful, but don't they say 'You can pick your friends but not your family'?*
Man, 68: General interviews, urban South

My wife died a year ago. I think life without her is very difficult. I don't really have anyone to talk to. Man, 78: Pakistani interviewee

. . . I had a husband who was brother, sister, uncle, mother, boyfriend, husband, father, everything . . . We knew each other from school . . . When that man died, if it was not God, if it was not God and the brethren supporting me from this church, I would be dead . . . Woman: Afro-Caribbean focus group

The participants who tended to feel most lonely and isolated, despite seeing care workers or neighbours almost every day, were those who had no relatives living in the UK. Some people had children or siblings who had emigrated during the 1950s and 1960s whom they had seldom seen since, although they wrote to each other and spoke regularly by telephone. Several participants felt particularly isolated at Christmas time, when they were aware that other older people were visiting or being visited by their families; for example, one woman whose only relatives lived in Australia had spent every Christmas alone for the past five years.

Migration

The consequences of migration were also a key area of discussion among the South Asian participants, although the issue was not referred to by the Afro-Caribbean participants. Community leaders and care workers who provided background information for the study suggested that this might be because most of the Afro-Caribbean men and women who took part in the study had migrated in the 1940s and 1950s, had not encountered a language barrier and had spent all their adult lives in the UK.

In general, South Asian participants were more recent migrants. Many of the women had not wanted to leave their families, and had never felt 'at home' in the UK; for some, their homesickness seemed to have been compounded by the death of family members overseas and by changes in their lives which were brought about by increased age:

. . . *after the death of my mother and father, he* [her husband] *did not allow me to go to Pakistan to see them or their graves. The loss of my parents, the only family I had of my own, took a lot out of me. These things have ongoing mental effects and are worse for the health than other illnesses.*

Woman, 56: Pakistani interviewee

When I first came to this country, things were really tough. I had no friends and I could not speak the language. My husband went to work seven days a week. I hardly ever saw him, but I had my children. My life was worth living then because I had my children. Now they have all grown up and gone their own ways. My youngest son lives with me and is not yet married, but he is out all day at work. I look forward to cooking for him, but I don't want to stop him from going out and having a good time. He is young. I feel that I just want to die in my sleep. I've lived my life. I lost my father and mother, and because of the children and financial reasons I could not go back to Bangladesh, so I only went back many years later to see just graves. Our lives are so difficult. Yet people back home say that you are living in England, but they have no idea what we have sacrificed for this. I did not want to come to this country, but I had no say in the matter. Two years ago my husband died. What have I got to look forward to? To me, it seems that I have already experienced death three times, once when I came to this country leaving all my family behind, once when my parents died and I could not be at their funerals, and once when my husband died. I just wanted to stop living . . .

Woman: Bangladeshi focus group

Whereas all the Afro-Caribbean women who took part in the study were still working or had worked until retirement, few of the South Asian women had worked outside the home. In some cases, their husbands did all the family shopping so that they had hardly any contact with the world beyond their own communities. Many were unable to speak English, and were non-literate in both English and their own languages; thus, they had no access to the English language media, and could not converse with English speakers. In consequence, many of the older South Asian women who took part in the study were completely isolated from the cultural life of the country in which they had spent much of their adult lives. Although interpreters and health advocates could help to some extent, older South Asian women had experienced problems when they had to attend the local hospital; most had South Asian GPs, but hospital consultants and nurses were less likely to be able to speak their languages. Older women were therefore afraid of getting lost and of being unable to explain their problem properly. Service providers and care workers who provided background information for the study pointed out that this leads to a high level of non-attendance for hospital appointments among older South Asian women. One informant described this as a 'vicious circle' in which older women agree to be referred by their GPs for tests at the hospital but, when the hospital contacts them, they destroy the letter or ignore the appointment. The women then present to their GP at a later date with the same symptoms, the GP refers them to the hospital and, again, they fail to attend. Informants argued that this not only wastes valuable NHS time and resources, but can have serious detrimental effects on the health of the women concerned.

2 Life events and personal circumstances

This section examines participants' beliefs about the way in which life events and personal circumstances might affect the health and wellbeing of older people. The following events and circumstances are discussed:

- caring for a partner or family member
- bereavement
- retirement
- past or present occupation

- mental health
- early life experiences.

Caring for a partner or family member

Participants found this a distressing topic for discussion; thus, focus group members were less willing to explore the issue than people who took part in interviews. The small number of Afro-Caribbean participants who were or had been carers did not report any adverse effects on their health and wellbeing. In the South Asian focus groups, the consequences for health and wellbeing of caring for elderly parents-in-law, and being cared for by one's daughter-in-law, were discussed at length, particularly amongst the female participants. In the general focus groups and interviews, being responsible for the care and support of a terminally ill or disabled family member was also felt to have a negative impact on health and wellbeing. Many participants felt that the experience of caring for a partner or relative over a long period of time in later life resulted in a decline in their own health. Participants made the following comments about this issue:

My wife died last year. She had cancer. I had so much help, from the family, the Marie Curie nurses, Macmillan nurses. But it had a terrible effect on my health. It was the emotional stress. It was like a physical pain, the feeling I couldn't do anything to help her . . .

Man, 76: General interviews, rural South

My wife had Alzheimer's. That had an effect on my health, oh, absolutely. I looked after her for four years. I couldn't leave her for more than half an hour. I felt ill, stressed. Man, 89: General interviews, urban Midlands

My responsibilities take priority over my health. I look after my mother-in-law and although my husband is now doing things for himself, his mother comes first.

Woman, 59: Bangladeshi interviewee

It's the worry, the stress. It's this feeling I'm responsible for three people, me and Mum and K—— [a brother with Down's syndrome]. It's like having all the worry and responsibility of kids too late in life. I know I'm stretching myself too far. I do all the washing and cleaning here, and then up at Mum's. K—— does his best, but he can't do much to help really, he's not well himself.

Woman, 62: General interviews, urban Midlands

I looked after my wife for ten years. She had senile dementia. I was used to heavy lifting so I managed somehow till I ruptured myself carrying her in here. She weighed 14 stone. I broke some of my teeth. That was gritting them when I lifted

her. I managed OK though, until I had the hernia.

Man, 84: General interviews, urban South

The majority of participants focused on the health consequences brought about by the stress of caring. However, a number of participants felt guilty about the resentment they felt towards the person they cared for:

I felt worn out, tired. It was trying. I got more asthma attacks. I felt angry with him and the situation. I got hardly any sleep. He wandered around at night, I had to be on call all the time.
Woman, 75: General interviews, rural South

The wife had MS. She couldn't get around much for years. I didn't cope very well, I used to lose my temper.
Man, 77: General interviews, rural Midlands

I shared looking after Mum and Dad with my sister. Life revolved around them. You have to live to someone else's routine. It's stressful, annoying, so there's a bit of guilt, temper, you get tetchy. When they died, I felt so guilty. I kept asking myself 'Did I give them enough time?'
Woman, 59: General interviews, urban Midlands

Some participants felt guilty because they had been relieved when the person they cared for died or was taken into hospital or a nursing home:

I had got to the stage where I couldn't go on any longer. He was incontinent and everything, and then he had a flu virus, and I'm afraid he didn't want to go into hospital, but he was only in hospital for six days . . . So I said 'Please keep him here until Christmas', so he was in there three weeks and of course it was marvellous, but then they put him out to [another hospital] and I didn't like it at all, but he was only in there for six nights and then he passed away . . . So at least he was only away for a month the whole time, but I had got to the stage where I couldn't cope with him anymore anyway.
Woman: 75+ focus group, urban North

While I feel very lost in the house on my own, at the same time I feel a sense of relief that it's over, that her pain is over, but also that it's over for me and that I don't have to look after her anymore. Then I feel guilty for feeling like that.
Man: 75+ focus group, urban North

Nevertheless, despite the negative health effects of being an older carer, some participants found that the experience enhanced their wellbeing, for example, as a result of having the constant companionship of a loved one. Furthermore, several men believed that caring for someone later in life had been a positive experience because they enjoyed the challenge, and it gave them a sense of purpose at a time when it seemed that their 'useful' life was coming to an end; for example, this man had cared for his terminally-ill wife:

In a funny sort of way, I enjoyed it. I mean, I didn't know anything about cooking, nothing like that, had to pick it up as I went along. I wasn't really looking forward to retiring. I carried on part time until she got really bad. But, d'you know, I was busier than when I was at work. I didn't know what to do with myself when she went into hospital.   Man, 76: General interviews, rural South

Bereavement

Many participants felt bereft of a special kind of easy and relaxed companionship when they lost their partner, or a friend or relative with whom they had lived for many years. Nevertheless, these feelings of loss and loneliness were, in many cases, tempered by relief and a sense of freedom, especially for some of the female participants. A quarter of the men and half of the women who took part in the study were widows. Several women spoke of the sense of freedom they derived from not having to cook meals three times a day, and both men and women enjoyed being able to do as they liked without having to defer to anyone else's wishes, for example:

No, it [his wife's death] *didn't have any effect on my health. Let's face it, in the end it was a relief for her and a relief for me. When my wife was alive, I had to consider what she wanted to do. Now I can do whatever I like, so long as I can afford to pay for it. I'd say the pattern of my life has changed, but not for the worse. I had a lot more to do then than I do now, the washing, the shopping, the cleaning.*
                    Man, 89: General interviews, urban South

In general, however, participants were saddened by the loss of their close companions, and a small number felt that they would 'never get over it'. The long-term effects of bereavement included loneliness and a feeling of depression, but the most common immediate response to the death of a spouse or close friend was to withdraw from social life. Some participants had become so withdrawn that they needed the help of friends, relatives or professional counsellors to recover. Participants made the following comments about this issue:

I shut myself in. I never went out except for my pension for over three months. I managed to pull myself together. I went over the Island [Isle of Wight]. *The people we went to every year invited me, gave me a free holiday. I still go to them twice a year and I reckon that helps me healthwise.*
                    Man, 84: General interviews, urban South

My friend died, she only lived over there. She was a lot older than me, she was like

a mother to me. It took a long time to get over it. It was like when my husband died, I didn't want to go out. Woman, 75: General interviews, rural Midlands

Although participants felt that bereavement affected their emotional wellbeing, only a small number of people felt that their physical health had been damaged by the death of someone close to them; for example, this woman attributed her worsening heart problems to grief following the death of her son:

Well, I was trying to take it very easy, but I was keeping crying and crying. So, one led to the other. Before, I used to keep going. From not sleeping, that is what do me heart. Woman, 79: Afro-Caribbean interviewee

Retirement

There were gender differences in beliefs about the way in which retirement from work has an impact on health and wellbeing. Male participants were more likely to report that they felt depressed after retirement than women, most of whom had welcomed it, or were looking forward to it, as an opportunity to pursue their own interests. In general, the health effects of retirement were thought to be influenced by the reason for retirement, that is, participants felt that being obliged to leave work early was more likely to lead to depression than leaving voluntarily, or at statutory retirement age. 'Early retirement' was often regarded as a euphemism for redundancy, and participants felt particularly bitter if they and their skills were dispensed with while younger and less well qualified staff were retained.

Some participants felt that older people could become isolated and lonely after retirement and it was also widely felt that, for men in particular, retirement could lead to such a decline in spirits and health that they died soon afterwards. In the experience of a number of male participants, being constantly in the company of their wives had led to arguments, especially if both partners were confined to the home by illness or disability. Among the female participants, some felt that their personal freedom was curtailed once their husbands retired; they had to account for their movements during the day and spend more time 'looking after' their husbands.

However, the majority of participants had enjoyed the period since they or their husbands had retired from work because although their incomes were reduced, it released them from the drudgery and stress of work. Many participants also enjoyed having more time to spend with their families and having the opportunity, often for the first time in their lives, to choose for themselves what to do each day. Participants made the following comments about retirement:

I don't think it's good for people to stop dead. They don't seem to last long after they retire.   Woman, 59: General interviews, urban Midlands

I've discovered a lot of people, as soon as they retire they become recluse. London is a lonely place if you have no one to communicate with, but by going to these clubs [for retired people] *you make friends and you have a social life.*
                                    Man, 70: Afro-Caribbean interviewee

I've really enjoyed it. This has been the best six years of my life, since I retired. I've got time to do as I like.   Man, 71: General interviews, rural North

Past or present occupation

Some of the oldest participants had been retired for many years; consequently, their previous occupation seemed to them to have little bearing on their present health experiences. However, a number of younger participants believed that a person's occupation could affect their health in later life, particularly if it brought them into contact with dust or dangerous chemicals, or put them at risk of accidents. In terms of their own personal experience, participants who felt that their health had been damaged by their working environment were generally women, unskilled or semi-skilled workers. Interviewees who felt that their health had been adversely affected by stress at work were generally men, managers, professionals or the owners of businesses. Participants made the following comments about this issue:

I worked in a rubber factory and they've proved the chemicals were dangerous. Some of the people I worked with have got chest problems, something to do with solvents.
                                    Man, 68: General interviews, urban South

People who worked at the same plant as me, though, because of the dust and powder we use, one or two people die and said they die of cancer. One or two people are sick now.   Man, 62: Afro-Caribbean interviewee

The stress, the responsibility. That can have an effect on your health. That can carry on after you leave work.   Man, 67: General interviews, rural South

You know them buffing machines that they use? I never understand properly how you get on with it to control it, and it run away and the cord tie up round me feet and me fell over and hit me back on concrete and from there it started.
                                    Woman, 62: Afro-Caribbean interviewee

Mental health

This issue was raised by a number of participants who felt that regardless of a person's state of physical health and mobility in later life, their wellbeing and quality of life could be affected by a decline in mental health. Participants did not believe that mental health problems were an inevitable consequence of ageing. Nevertheless, many participants in the general and Afro-Caribbean samples associated Alzheimer's disease and senile dementia with old age and were fearful of developing these conditions because of the implications for independence, self-control and dignity. Participants made the following comments about this issue:

I looked after my mother. She was mentally confused. She couldn't look after herself, couldn't wash herself. I don't want to be the same burden on anybody.

Woman, 79: General interviews, rural North

I dread getting Alzheimer's, not being in control of myself. I wouldn't even mind being disabled as long as I was mentally OK.

Woman, 63: General interviews, rural Midlands

Some participants had suffered mental health problems, such as depression, but had not realised that they were ill until their friends or relatives urged them to seek medical advice. This finding suggests that mental health problems among older people may be exacerbated by lack of social support. Mental health problems were associated with bereavement and with personal circumstances such as marital problems or being a carer:

Well, I had a nervous breakdown. Other people noticed I was depressed, but I didn't
Woman, 59: General interviews, urban South

My friend at the Volunteer Bureau, she said she thought I had depression. I said 'You're mad', but she went on and on so in the end I went to the doctor. I said to him 'I don't know why I'm here' and he said 'I do, you've got depression'. I had tablets, and the sleeping tablets, and I did feel better . . .

Man, 77: General interviews, rural Midlands

Participants believed that there is less sympathy for, and understanding of, mental health problems than other forms of ill health, even among the medical profession. Some participants spoke of the difficulties they encountered in obtaining a diagnosis for a relative with symptoms of Alzheimer's disease or senile dementia. In a number of cases, symptoms of serious degenerative mental health problems were dismissed by GPs as a 'natural' feature of the ageing process; thus, relatives felt they were being denied the assistance they needed, for example:

Alzheimer's, that's a very different thing, that's not like being ill-ill. The doctor wouldn't admit my husband had it, not for years. He could see him going downhill, behaving not himself. We hardly got any help, not like they do these days.

Woman, 75: General interviews, rural South

South Asian participants believed that health was the product of an interaction between the physical and the spiritual and mental aspects of their lives; thus, many believed that there is a relationship between physical health and mental health problems such as depression. Participants made the following comments about this issue:

I think my health has been affected the most by my physical illness. My spiritual sense is still strong although I find that meditating is not as easy as it used to be. With my physical problems having increased, I now find myself mentally disturbed too, feeling cross with myself for not being able to do as much. I feel as if I have become a cabbage. Man, 78: Indian interviewee

I know that it might sound strange, but worry is one of the biggest problems and also one of the biggest causes of illness. Stress is caused by day-to-day life events that take over your whole being. You can't eat properly, you can't sleep and what's more, you don't feel like doing anything. Man, 70: Bangladeshi interviewee

Some Afro-Caribbean participants also mentioned disturbed sleep in the context of mental health problems, and felt that the quality of one's sleep in later life can affect health and wellbeing. Participants felt that spiritual and mental health are closely related; thus, having a 'troubled conscience' leads to nightmares which are the principle cause of disturbed sleep:

When you go to bed and you can't sleep, that's your conscience because you've done something wrong. You are never in peace, never. Happens to us all, your conscience rules your mind. Man, 62: Afro-Caribbean interviewee

I have trouble sleeping. When I go to sleep, I dream a lot of stupidness, it's frightening. I dream about people who have died, have conversations with them.

Man, 79: Afro-Caribbean interviewee

Early life experiences

A number of participants felt that experiences in childhood, such as physical cruelty, deprivation and an inadequate diet, could have an effect on health in later life. South Asian participants spoke at most length about this issue:

In India when I was a young girl we were very poor. We did not have proper food, not like people have here. There was no drinking water that was clean. We lived off very basic foods and we had to work hard in the fields all day. This has affected my health. When I came to this country . . . I was suffering from many illnesses. At the time when you are young, illnesses can be managed but it catches up with you in your old age.   Woman, 87: Indian interviewee

Health is affected by many things. For me I think it was at the beginning poverty. I'm from a poor background. While you are young you can manage yourself and carry on, but as you get older you can feel the strain. And then one day it catches up with you and you find that you have all these illnesses, but by then it is too late.

Woman, 56: Pakistani interviewee

3 Personal behaviour

This section investigates the extent to which participants felt that people's past and present behaviour affects their health and wellbeing in later life. Discussion focused mainly on the effects on health of eating, smoking and drinking alcohol.

Diet and nutrition

Participants believed that nutrition is one of the most important influences on health and wellbeing throughout life; for example, loss of appetite was regarded as a major symptom of ill health. Furthermore, eating snack foods and eating irregularly were thought to cause health problems, for example:

My diet suffers because I can't eat properly when I'm working [as a home carer]. *I don't have time in the day to eat properly. I snack on the move in between clients, biscuits, sandwiches, no proper lunch-hour.*

Woman, 59: Afro-Caribbean interviewee

In general, the men and women who took part in the study perceived eating and drinking as social activities; they were extremely interested in food and spoke at great length about their eating habits. Most believed that eating regular meals gave structure to their day, and several found cooking an enjoyable pastime. Although some participants felt that they were unable to afford a good-quality diet, the majority believed that they were eating nutritious food and in sufficient quantities to satisfy their appetites. Indeed, a number of participants, especially those who were housebound, spent a large proportion of their income on food. In some cases, people felt that there was little else in their lives that gave them as much pleasure as eating and drinking their favourite things, including sweets, chocolates, wine and spirits:

'A little of what you fancy does you good', that's what they say . . . I think there's too much advice and banning things. I think it's up to the person to decide what's

good and bad and make their own choice.

Woman, 75: General interviews, rural South

Yes, I am ill, but at the end of the day, I can't give up my food. I mean, you only live once. Woman: Pakistani focus group

In general, participants felt that they knew what constitutes a 'good' and 'bad' diet, for example, that fruit and vegetables are beneficial and that items such as chocolates and cakes are unlikely to promote good health. However, non-diabetic participants generally felt that, at their age, little harm was likely to result from indulging in 'treats' containing high levels of sugar and fat as long as they also ate plenty of fibre, vegetables and fruit. The majority of participants in the general and Afro-Caribbean samples felt that there was no harm in drinking alcohol in moderation, or even having the occasional 'binge'. Some had seen recent media reports that a glass of red wine a day is good for health; others felt that a drink before bedtime gave them a better night's sleep. Many people felt that having a drink with friends was an important feature of their social lives, and particularly enjoyed wine with meals and visits to pubs and clubs.

In studies involving people of all ages, Calnan (1987; 1990; 1994) found that there were class differences in beliefs about the nutritional value of different types of food. For example, he found that working-class women believed that meals should be 'substantial and filling', whereas middle-class women placed more emphasis on 'a balanced diet' and 'everything in moderation' (1990: p. 74); he found that both groups believed it was important to eat fresh rather than processed or packaged food. In the present study, regional differences were more marked than class differences, with participants from all social groups in the North placing more emphasis on the importance of having hot meals. Researchers attributed this difference to the weather in the North of England, where it snowed heavily during the period when most of the research was carried out.

In the present study, participants also differed in their attitudes regarding the nutritional value of processed foods. Many men and women from the general sample, particularly those in the older age groups, argued that packaged meals are more convenient, more economical and just as nutritious as meals cooked 'from scratch' using fresh ingredients. A large number of participants, particularly in the older age groups, were using microwave ovens for most of their cooking and found that heating ready-made meals involved them in less standing and used far less fuel; in addition, the small portions and strong flavours of many ready-meals suited those with smaller appetites and a reduced sense of taste and smell. A further bonus for older and frailer participants was that a week's meals were light to carry and could be stored in a small freezer or cupboard. The consensus view was that processed foods benefit older people's health because without the convenience of ready-meals and the microwave, many people would probably live on soup and sandwiches.

Widowed female participants particularly enjoyed having the option of using convenience foods after many years of cooking meals for their husbands and families. However, the majority of participants who made extensive use of processed and microwaved meals believed that it was important to supplement their diet with fresh fruit and vegetables. Overall, this set of findings suggests that there is a contradiction between beliefs and behaviour. Participants believed that a nutritionally balanced diet is important yet their comments suggested that they would be willing to forgo the health benefits of a cooked meal if this involved them in too much expense or effort.

There was more support for the findings by Calnan (1987; 1990; 1994) among Afro-Caribbean participants, most of whom believed that fresh food is more nutritious than processed food. Nevertheless, a number of people believed that fresh food is of lower quality in the UK than in the West Indies, and has probably been tampered with in some way:

In the West Indies, you could get fresh callaloo, fresh everything, they didn't mix it with anything, but here, everything they mix it. Look at the fish. Sometimes I say 'God, you made the fish in the sea and they do their own thing'. Now, they take out of the fish whatsoever God put inside of them and put it in a pan and inject them . . . and they have no taste, see what I mean? They don't allow the fish to do as they did before, they're trying to do it for them.

Woman: Afro-Caribbean focus group

Among the older South Asian men and women who took part in the study, discussion of the impact of diet and food on health was influenced, in many cases, by the belief that certain foods have therapeutic properties. In a study of the health beliefs of British Bangladeshis in relation to diabetes, Greenhalgh, Helman and Chowdhury (1998) found that some foods were perceived as being more digestible, nourishing and strengthening than others, particularly for older people:

'"Strong" foods, perceived as energy-giving, included white sugar (in solid form), lamb, beef, ghee (derived from butter), solid fat and spices. Such foods were considered health-giving and powerful for the healthy body but liable to produce worsening of illness in those debilitated by age or illness. "Weak" foods, preferred in the everyday menu and for the old or infirm, included boiled (pre-fluffed) rice and cereals.

The digestibility of food was considered to be related to the cooking method, with boiled and steamed foods classified as easy to digest and raw, fried or baked foods hard to digest. The former were considered suitable for the elderly, infirm and young while the latter were preferred for healthy adults.'

Greenhalgh, Helman and Chowdhury
(1998: amended version from *BMJ* website)

Similar beliefs about the properties of food were expressed by a number of participants in the present study, several of whom also spoke in terms of 'hot' and 'cold' foods. Bhopal (1986) found that 'hot' and 'cold' foods were used to treat earache, toothache and stomach-ache. In the present study, lamb's trotters were thought to be a 'hot' and 'strengthening' food which relieves the symptoms of rheumatism:

I make sure that I have my daughter-in-law cook me lamb trotters once a week. These have a lot of strength in them. You need all the strength that you can get when you are getting old.   Man: Bangladeshi focus group

In general, South Asian participants felt that good quality food, together with the activities of cooking for the family and eating meals together, promotes wellbeing. However, some participants felt that they were probably buying, cooking and eating more food than was good for health, and several men and women had digestive and cardiovascular problems which their GPs had told them were caused by too much fatty and heavily spiced food.

Habits

Participants believed that habits such as drinking alcohol, smoking tobacco and taking drugs could have negative effects on the health of people of all ages. None of the men and women who took part in the study felt that they were consuming too much alcohol. However, a small number of people believed that they were probably addicted to sleeping tablets, and many participants from the general and South Asian samples smoked. None of the members of the Afro-Caribbean sample were current smokers.

A number of participants were ex-smokers and, of these, the majority had stopped smoking on a sudden whim without experiencing any major 'withdrawal' symptoms; several men and women used the same terminology to describe how they gave up, that is, 'I just woke up one morning and didn't want to do it anymore'. In a small number of cases, participants had given up smoking because they had bronchial or heart problems, or because they could no longer afford it; in an equally small number of cases, participants continued to smoke despite having serious cardiovascular problems.

Calnan (1994) argues that material circumstances are a major influence on smoking habits. Citing a study by Graham (1987) of women's smoking habits, Calnan points out that low-income households tend to spend more on tobacco products than other households, and argues that 'smoking reflects the social isolation of caring for children in poverty' (p. 80). Calnan (1994) also cites a study by Calnan and Williams (1991) of the salience of health for a wide range of age groups; his comments reflect the opinions and beliefs of many of the smokers from lower socioeconomic groups who took part in the present study:

> '. . . smoking appeared to be used by working-class women as a resource for relaxation and for handling the stresses and strains of everyday life. In contrast, all of the men who smoked stressed the habitual and sociable nature of smoking.'
>
> Calnan (1994: p. 81)

Current smokers who took part in the present study had an ambivalent attitude towards the habit; most acknowledged that it was probably bad for their health, yet none was prepared to give it up. Some felt defiant in the face of so much criticism of the habit, and refused to give up. Others felt that their health had not been damaged at all by smoking or, conversely, that their health had been irreparably damaged so there did not seem any point in giving up. Some people felt that smoking was one of the few pleasures they had in their lives, and others smoked 'for something to do'. A number of participants, notably women, smoked because they felt it helped them to cope with problems or unpleasant living circumstances. Some South Asian participants smoked for therapeutic reasons, for example, to aid digestion; furthermore, smoking was often perceived as a social activity among the South Asian participants, and was carried out in a group setting with other men or women. Participants made the following comments about smoking:

It's the only thing I've got left to do when I am in the flat on my own. I can't see the point in giving it up now.　　　　Woman: 75+ focus group, urban South

I'm not making excuses, but I think if I could leave that flat I would give up

smoking just like that.   Woman: 55–64 focus group, London

I smoke about fifteen cigarettes a day and I'd not stop for health reasons, only if I couldn't afford it. I reckon God'll take me smoking or not when the time's right.
                    Woman, 74: General interviews, urban North

I have smoked all my life. When I came to this country I brought my hookah with me from Pakistan. The reason that I smoke is because I suffer from indigestion, and I find that the hookah twice a day after meals aids my digestion. I only smoke in my own home and in the homes of my wider family, but I never smoke outside, it's not womanly to smoke outside. My husband doesn't like me and his Mum smoking because he doesn't smoke, so when he comes into the house we go into the next room and hide from him, even though he knows what we are doing.
                                        Woman: Pakistani focus group

After we have finished eating, the men all sit together and will usually have a cigarette. It is a socialising thing more than anything else . . . After a cigarette, they will ask for tea and then us ladies sit and have tea as well.
                                    Woman, 72: Pakistani focus group

3 Control over health in later life

This chapter investigates the extent to which the older people who took part in the study believed they had control over their present and future state of health. As Chapters 1 and 2 demonstrate, individual health beliefs and behaviours are influenced not only by personal circumstances and experiences but by a wide range of social and cultural factors, including beliefs about the social worth of older people and expectations about how they should behave. For example, older people may internalise the view that the elderly have less social value than younger people and therefore have less claim on valuable and scarce resources such as good quality housing and health care. They may also internalise the view that old age is a period of life in which they must expect to experience more ill health, decreased mobility and a steady decline in their mental faculties. Furthermore, older people's behaviour may be influenced by the view that, in later life, it is inappropriate for people to retain control over their own lives, or to be active, lively and exuberant.

The health locus of control thesis seeks to explain health-related behaviour in terms of individuals' beliefs about the level of control they have over their health rather than in terms of the degree to which they believe they are at risk of disease; if individuals feel that they have little control over their health, this may discourage them from following health promotion advice. Calnan (1994) provides the following explanation of the health locus of control thesis:

> 'This construct consists of three different dimensions of belief about the source of control of health: the internal, powerful other, and chance. People who score high on the internal scale are more likely to believe that health is the result of their own behavior, while high scores on the other two suggest either that health depends on the power of doctors or on chance, fate, or luck.'
>
> Calnan (1994: p. 70)

Regardless of class, location, age and level of education, everyone who took part in the present study believed that chance, or God, plays some part in determining health in later life. Participants from the general population believed that health is largely determined by luck, whereas men and women from the South Asian and Afro-Caribbean samples tended to believe that the 'powerful other' (Calnan, 1994: p. 70) who ultimately controls their health is God. In addition, a few participants from the South Asian and Afro-Caribbean samples believed that other people could take control of their health by casting 'the evil eye' on them, that is, by conjuring up malign spiritual forces to bring about ill health or death. For example, this woman had a form of diabetes but believed that her symptoms resulted from being cursed by an enemy:

I suffered from the evil eye of a woman in my village when I was younger and since that day I have not been able to eat sugar. Because of this all my life I have suffered from intense dizziness in the morning when I get up. When I try to explain to the doctor that I am suffering for a particular reason, he does not listen to me but will say that I need a scan. He has given me many different tablets . . . I take them not to disappoint him but I throw them away. I know what my illness is.

Woman: Indian focus group

In general, however, participants believed that some older people have worse health than others because 'the odds were stacked against them from the start', for example, by being born into a poor family or a family with a genetic predisposition to diseases such as cancer. Likewise, through no fault of their own, some people's health has been irreparably damaged because they had accidents, caught contagious diseases or lived and worked in dirty, polluted environments. Participants made the following comments about this issue:

I really used to take care of myself and look at me now. I think it's all a matter of luck.   Man, 89: General interviews, urban Midlands

There are genetic factors involved. My family have a history of heart disease and then I suffered from angina, and the doctors related it to that. But I say it is from God.   Woman, 63: Bangladeshi interviewee

Anyone could take sick any time. It could be in the family bloodstream, later in life you get it. I could cross the road and a car knock me down.

Man, 62: Afro-Caribbean interviewee

When we get sick, we just get sick. We each have our moments to be sick, it's just the way it is. There are some older people who are pretty strong when they move around. Well, that's just destiny, I put it down to that.

Man, 79: Afro-Caribbean interviewee

Nevertheless, some participants believed that behaviour could affect health; thus, drug addicts, alcoholics and heavy smokers 'tempt fate', or squander the gift of good health that God has given them:

. . . you can't blame God for being a druggy, an alcoholic . . .

Man, 77: General interviews, rural Midlands

Furthermore, there were differences in attitude in terms of age, and of educational achievement. Many of the South Asian participants could not speak fluent English and several were non-literate in English and in their own languages. Some participants from higher socioeconomic groups had experienced poverty and deprivation in child-hood; most had left school without qualifications between the ages of 12 and 15, although a few had later acquired educational or professional qualifications at 'night school'. Thus, a number of the participants were 'self-made' men and women in terms of socioeconomic status, and several other participants from lower socioeconomic groups were, by their own definition, 'self-educated'. In interviews in particular, younger participants and those with a higher level of education generally took the view that health in later life is determined by individual behaviour coupled with luck or the will of God. Thus, it is possible to improve one's quality of life and general wellbeing by paying careful attention to diet and exercise, even though it may not be possible to prevent ill health altogether since this is a matter of chance or is preordained by God or fate:

There are things that we can do that may mean that we will be healthier and live longer, you know, like being careful about what we eat, and exercising. But I think that at the end of the day it is something that is very much in God's hands. When everyone has come with a fixed time in this world, and when this life will end, when it has been prescribed, then how can this be changed? It can't, can it?

Man, 59: Pakistani interviewee

However, other participants generally felt that with the exception of minor illnesses such as colds, there is little the individual can do to influence his or her health in later life. Thus, it is better to let medical experts deal with health matters:

. . . I can take care of myself by taking the medication that the doctor has prescribed, by doing as the doctor says, but theoretically I am not the one who can control anything. Age plays a large part as well as background, and then finally it is God who does as he wants.   Woman, 66: Bangladeshi interviewee

He is the doctor and he must know best. You could be dying and you don't know. He will know and send you to the hospital for a blood test . . . a check-up, x-ray or anything.   Woman, 62: Afro-Caribbean interviewee

You don't have to risk your health. You take the doctor's advice, you put yourself into their hands, that's what they're for. I always take all the tablets if they give them me.
Woman, 75: General interviews, urban South

I rely on the doctor to keep me going. I don't do anything to make myself healthier.
Man, 88: General interviews, urban South

In comparison, younger participants, particularly those from the general sample, felt that doctors are not infallible and that each individual is the 'expert' on his or her own body; thus, although people may not be able to prevent illnesses from occurring, they should retain as much control as possible over their medical treatment. Participants made the following comments about this issue:

I think I'm assertive when it comes to doctors. I insist they give me all the facts.
Woman, 59: General interviews, urban Midlands

They're not gods, you know. It's my body. I want them to tell me exactly what's going on.
Woman, 58: General interviews, urban South

The majority of participants felt that although they had little ultimate control over their health in older age, they were 'in control' in other areas of their lives. However, a number of participants felt that they had little control over anything that happened to them; these tended to be South Asian women, and men and women from the oldest age groups:

The doctor told me to eat just boiled foods, rather than curries and greasy food, but I feel as if I should not bother anyone to cook a separate meal for me, so I eat what everyone else eats. My daughter-in-law already has a lot to do. Why should I burden her with the additional problem?
Woman: Pakistani focus group

I think whatever we live through is destined for us. If we try and fight it, we will just end up upsetting ourselves.
Woman, 67: Indian interviewee

Whatever happens comes from God as a test in life, for us to show God that we remember Him. If we were happy all the time, we would never remember God. Everything is from Him and that is what I believe in.
Woman, 63: Bangladeshi interviewee

I don't have any control over what I eat. We just get given a menu in the home.
Woman, 72 (in residential care): General interviews, urban North

Have I got control over my health? No, my health's in control of me.
Man, 80: General interviews, rural North

Summary

In Part 1, we examined older people's beliefs about health and the factors which affect health in later life. We then moved on to consider the extent to which older people feel they are in control of their health. Here, we focused on investigating whether or not participants believed that people can influence their health in later life through their own behaviour. Our findings indicate that the older men and women who took part in the study shared the view of Ginn, Arber and Cooper

(1997) that 'many of the causes of ill health are outside the individual's control' (p. 34). While a small number of participants believed that ageist attitudes and ageist social policies influence people's experience of health in later life, all believed that health in older age is ultimately a matter of 'luck', 'fate' or 'the will of God'. However, when the data were analysed, factors which participants attributed to 'chance' or 'fate' could be traced back to their socioeconomic and environmental circumstances, or to cultural traditions regarding the way in which older people should behave or be treated in their various communities.

Nevertheless, although participants believed that people ultimately have little control over their state of health in later life, many felt that quality of life can be improved and wellbeing enhanced in older age by practising certain 'healthy' behaviours. Paradoxically, however, not all of those who believed that 'behaving healthily' was good for them were putting these beliefs into practice. This issue is discussed in more detail in Part 2.

Part 2

Older people's health promotion behaviour

In Part 1, we discussed the wide range of socioeconomic, environmental and cultural factors which participants in the study believed could have a negative effect on older people's health.

In Part 2, we investigate the extent to which the older men and women who took part in the study practise health-promoting behaviours, and identify the sources from which they obtain their information about health. We then examine the factors which encourage older people to comply with health promotion advice, or deter them from 'behaving healthily'.

4 'Healthy behaviour' in older age

This chapter examines the ways in which the older men and women who took part in the study defined healthy behaviour, and the importance which they attached to having a 'healthy lifestyle'. Many of the participants believed that although it may not be possible to prevent ill health altogether in later life, 'behaving healthily' can enhance well-being, for example by improving mobility and making people less susceptible to minor ailments such as coughs and colds. However, although a number of participants made scathing comments about individuals who 'tempt fate' by neglecting themselves or practising 'risky' behaviours such as smoking, the majority believed that people should be free to do as they please with their own bodies.

Participants defined healthy behaviour in later life as doing one's best to achieve any or all of the following:

- remaining mentally and physically active
- having a nutritionally well-balanced diet
- eating and drinking in moderation
- avoiding 'risky' behaviours such as smoking
- having a 'positive mental attitude'
- interacting regularly with other people
- consulting a medical practitioner about worrying symptoms
- having regular routine health checks
- following expert medical advice.

The importance of 'behaving healthily' in later life

The importance which participants attached to healthy behaviour varied considerable from person to person, and was often linked to the experience of ill health. For example, one interviewee in her early 70s who had recently had a mastectomy believed it was essential for her health to play tennis and take part in exercise classes several times a week. Other women of a similar age who had not had major health problems felt that doing their household chores was sufficient exercise:

I go up and down the stairs all day. If that is not exercise then I don't know what i
Woman: Bangladeshi focus group

Likewise, people who had experienced digestive or cardiovascular problems, or diabetes, attached more importance to the whole family eating a carefully balanced diet than people who had not shared these experiences:

Many of our people eat very greasy, fatty foods . . . We used to as well. It is only after my angina attack that everything has changed. I now use skimmed milk. I use very little oil in my cooking and I have stopped eating red meat completely. I eat a lot more fish now, mainly mackerel. I don't like the taste of this but I was told by the dietitian that this particular fish is very good for lowering the level of cholesterol in your body, so I eat it like taking medicine. The family has even stopped eating things like fresh cream cakes because of me.

Woman, 56: Pakistani interviewee

I don't listen to what they say on the telly and in the paper, it's a load of nonsense. I eat beef and fish and I like a cigarette. I won't stop. I've never changed my diet. It's my way of life.   Woman, 60: General interviews, urban North

Making changes in health-related behaviour

Other participants who did not have health problems had tried to make an effort to live a healthier lifestyle, but had failed to maintain the changes, for example, in trying to eat a more balanced diet:

You do it for a while and then you tend to forget and just go ahead and eat what you want.   Man: 55–64 focus group, urban North

You miss not eating the things you enjoy but are supposed to be bad for you and so after a while you slip back into eating them again.

Woman: 65–74 focus group, urban North

Many participants resolved this dilemma by moderating their intake of foodstuffs which they considered were bad for health in large quantities. This strategy was felt to be more manageable than cutting out certain foods altogether, and such explanations were often accompanied by the maxims 'A little of what you fancy does you good', and 'Everything in moderation'. However, other participants offset failure to make health-related changes in one area with additional efforts in areas where they had been more successful, a tactic which was also observed in a study of health and behavioural change carried out by Hunt and McLeod (1987, cited in Calnan, 1994). In the present study, this participant had tried and failed to give up smoking:

I've been smoking since my teens . . . I gave up after my hysterectomy but it's fashionable to smoke in my age group, you know. All my friends called to see me, puffing away, and I started again . . . I counteract it by being healthy, taking the dogs for walks, swimming. Woman, 59: General interviews, urban Midlands

However, a small number of participants felt that their attempts to make health-related changes in one area of their lives were causing problems in others, for example:

Now at home I insist that by 12 o'clock midday the curries are ready. I will have my lunch at around 12.30. With my lunch I have one cigarette, then I go to sleep. In the evening again I have a proper cooked meal and again I have one cigarette. I am trying to give up smoking, you see, which is why I am eating a lot more, but I think I am putting on weight and will not stop smoking anyway.

Man, 75: Pakistani interviewee

This man felt that he was suffering the consequences now, in older age, of not having made behavioural changes in the past:

Healthy behaviour is very important, but I realise now that you need to take care of yourself throughout your life to minimise the chances of ill health in later life. If you look after yourself by eating regularly, not doing to your body what you should not, like abusing it, then things are OK. I was silly. I smoked too much, whatever I could get my hands on to tell you the truth, and now I can hardly breathe without coughing. My asthma will be the end of me, I know this, but I have no one to blame.

Man, 74: Indian interviewee

Some of the female South Asian participants also felt that there were cultural barriers to healthy behaviour such as taking purposeful exercise. However, the community leaders and care workers who provided background information for the study pointed out that many younger South Asian women take part in women-only swimming sessions and exercise classes in the area where the research took place; thus, it may well be that these views are held mainly by older people in the community, or that this woman was unaware of the local facilities:

Our women do not exercise, but I think that they should. It is seen as something that is wrong, you know, something that is Western. I suppose our way of life is different from the English people, but exercise can be done by anybody. But also our women do not have time to exercise, what with homes and families.

Woman, 67: Pakistani interviewee

Nevertheless, there were some participants who felt that they had always led 'healthy' lives, or had successfully incorporated health-promoting behaviours into their lifestyles. In general, participants had managed to establish new habits because they were encouraged by experiencing positive changes in their health and wellbeing. One man in his late 80s who had been unable to rise from his chair without assistance before joining an exercise class was now able to walk to the shops; this man and his wife, who had recently taken up allotment gardening, had noticed health benefits in terms of mobility, diet and wellbeing:

. . . doing the ploughing and the turning over of the soil help to bring your muscles

and other parts of the body into play. It's so rewarding when I goes to get the fresh vegetables. Man, 70: Afro-Caribbean interviewee

Other participants reported improvements in their health as a result of making modest behavioural changes, such as continuing to eat much the same diet as before but substituting low-fat products where possible and adding fibre-rich cereals, nuts, pulses and fresh fruit and vegetables:

Healthy behaviour is doing all those things which will keep you feeling and looking good. I think it is important at this age that we are extra careful about what we eat. Both my husband and I are on high-fibre and low-fat diets.
Woman, 64: Indian interviewee

In terms of remaining physically and mentally active, many people quoted the maxims 'Use it or lose it', and 'You rust out before you wear out', for example:

Well, I look at it [the body] *as iron, and things like that get corroded if it is not used, so therefore you keep turning over, keep turning over, and you avoid corrosion.*
Man, 70: Afro-Caribbean interviewee

The importance of 'positive mental attitude'

Most of the activities which participants defined as healthy behaviour were relevant to the health and wellbeing of people of any age. However, participants felt that it was particularly important for the promotion of good health in later life to mix with other people on a regular basis, and to maintain a 'positive mental attitude'. These two aspects of healthy behaviour were believed to be closely related since people with nothing to look forward to, such as visits from friends and family, or social outings, were likely to become depressed, lethargic and less inclined to take care of themselves or to seek companionship. Furthermore, people with a negative outlook on life were often spurned as companions by others; for example, many participants said that they avoided the company of other older people who, in their opinion, 'moaned too much' or were 'miseries'. Participants made the following comments about this issue:

What I call healthy behaviour, getting up and doing what you have to do. Good wash or a bath, tidy yourself and go out and get fresh air, getting your circulation going. Man, 79: Afro-Caribbean interviewee

In feeling positive about yourself, you feel healthy. You know, when you strive to make

the most of everything, this is all part of being healthy. Just basic things like combing your hair regularly, changing your clothes and washing make you feel so much better.   Woman, 58: Bangladeshi interviewee

Some people are, well, I would call them lazy . . . Some people just sit down, sit down. They think of nothing to do . . . I come across people like that. Sitting doing nothing makes your health worse because your blood is not circulating.
                    Woman, 79: Afro-Caribbean interviewee

I think you can get into bad habits when you live on your own. There's a danger you'll let yourself go. I think if you look smart you'll behave smart. You know when you're in your old gardening clothes and you think 'I'll just pop down the shops', and you keep your head down praying you don't meet anyone you know? Well, it's like that. You feel smart, you can keep your head up and look people in the eye.
                    Man, 76: General interviews, rural South

Seeking medical advice

In Chapter 3, it was noted that some of the older men and women who took part in the study felt that their medical advisers were 'in control' of their health. However, it was not always the case that the practitioners consulted by participants were qualified in Western medicine. Many of the Bangladeshi, Pakistani and Indian participants had consulted practitioners of traditional South Asian medicine, as had a small number of participants from the general sample. Several members of the general sample had also consulted acupuncturists, practitioners of traditional Chinese herbal medicine, aromatherapists, homoeopaths and hypnotherapists. However, all the members of the Afro-Caribbean sample relied primarily on 'conventional' medicine, except in the case of minor ailments such as colds when they usually tried West Indian herbal remedies before consulting their GPs; these remedies, collectively known as 'bush', are herb and plant extracts brewed like tea or made into a cordial.

Although the majority of Afro-Caribbean participants were pleased with the service they received from their GPs and from the hospital service, there was a degree of reluctance to consult their GPs among members of the general sample as a result of perceived ageism; this issue is discussed in Chapter 6. South Asian participants were generally satisfied with the medical services they received. However, although all the older men and women who took part in the study had South Asian GPs, some of the female participants felt that this did not necessarily make their doctors more understanding of their problems, for example:

Like I said, I only go to the GP when I am desperate. Although she is a Pakistani woman herself she pretends she does not know about our culture or ways of living. Education does this to people sometimes . . . Because of her attitude, our ladies are suffering . . . The only reason I'm still with her practice is because it is the nearest to my house. I don't drive and if the doctor's surgery were far away I would have problems. Woman, 60: Pakistani interviewee

Nevertheless, community leaders and health workers who provided background information for the study pointed out that medical practitioners are generally so highly regarded in the South Asian community that they are consulted for every incidence of ill health, however minor. One of the participants made the same point, arguing that she thought people should be prepared to take more responsibility for looking after their own health:

As well as using the GP, I think one must look at prevention, about what you can do to improve your health. Most of our Asian people will just go to the doctor even if they have a flu. Woman, 64: Indian interviewee

Indeed, a large number of South Asian participants indicated that they did not feel that they had received 'proper' treatment if they were given health promotion advice by their GP rather than a prescription. Thus, when participants spoke of 'advice' from their GP, they generally meant following the instructions they were given about taking medication:

Healthy behaviour is eating properly, doing as the doctor says, about taking medication regularly. Woman, 58: Bangladeshi interviewee

I think if I eat properly, and when I am ill if I go to the doctor, then it is fine. When the doctor gives advice people should take it, this is part of healthy behaviour. Woman, 67: Pakistani interviewee

However, some participants, notably men, preferred to try traditional South Asian remedies instead of, or in conjunction with, Western medicine by using herbal medicaments or by visiting a South Asian healer; Hindu and Sikh participants consulted their guru (spiritual adviser) and Muslim participants consulted a Pir (spiritual healer). Participants made the following comments about this issue:

. . . there are certain illnesses like flu and stomachache that can be cured by herbal remedies, but the doctor will not tell you the herbal remedies. Woman, 66: Pakistani interviewee

I only go to my GP if I feel to be suffering from something serious. Other than this, my family have so many herbal remedies which are passed down from generation to

generation that anything minor is cured by using different herbs.

Man, 73: Indian interviewee

I was so ill and I had visited my GP almost every two days in a week, but there was no relief. My stomach had started to swell and the doctor did not really know why. After all, they do learn all their information from books, don't they? They are not really gifted or anything. Then one of my relatives told me about this Pir who could cure many illnesses, but he was all the way in Birmingham. Because of the level of pain I was experiencing, my husband decided that he would take me to this Pir. He charged us £200 for half an hour of his time. He asked me what was wrong and then made me two different amulets, one to tie on my arm and one to drink twice a day. He did not explain my illness to me but after taking the medicine for two weeks I was completely cured. It was as if it was a miracle. The Pirs are gifted people. I recommend him to everyone now.   Woman: Pakistani focus group

. . . if I have problems or there is something that I do not understand then I go to my guru and then if advised by my guru I would go to the doctor.

Man, 72: Indian interviewee

Screening and routine check-ups

Many participants from the general and Afro-Caribbean samples regularly attended 'well-person' clinics; however, the availability of this type of service varied between areas and regions. For example, almost every participant in the urban South sample had access to 'well-person' checks and were contacted by their GP if they did not attend the surgery at least once a year; in a number of cases, frail or very elderly participants were visited regularly at home by their GPs. This was certainly not the case in other areas, and far fewer participants in the rural South and rural North samples knew of or attended 'well-person' clinics than in other regions.

A large number of women from the general and Afro-Caribbean samples said that they were regularly attending for screening tests such as mammograms and cervical smears, or would be willing to attend if they were asked. However, many women pointed out that there is an upper age limit for screening tests:

I'd go for all the tests and that if they called me, but they don't bother calling you when you get to a certain age. It's 65 or so for mammograms and I found my lump years after that.   Woman, 72: General interviews, rural South

South Asian community leaders and health workers who provided background information for the study told researchers that they had recently held a series of 'health workshops' at the mosque serving the area where the research was carried out. Many local men and women took part in discussions about health matters such as screening and nutrition. Nevertheless, although some of the older South Asian women who took part in the study had attended the workshops, most were reluctant to take advantage of screening opportunities or 'well-person' checks because they did not wish to expose their bodies to strangers and could not see the point in having tests if they had no symptoms:

I have never been for breast screening because there is nothing wrong with me and neither have I had a cervical smear test done. I don't like the idea of people just touching my body. And besides, these doctors in the hospitals just use people as guinea pigs.   Woman, 60: Pakistani interviewee

When my appointment for breast screening came through I just threw it away. What's the point? You just stand naked in front of a man who feels you in embarrassing places. I had a friend who went because her daughter made her go and she said that she would die but never go back to have herself checked. She said she could have died of embarrassment when they were touching her all over. I mean, your breasts are a very personal part of your body. It's not like showing your leg or arm.   Woman: Bangladeshi focus group

However, many of the South Asian men said that they would be willing to have any checks that were offered to them:

Of course I go to any check-up. At the end of the day, it is for my benefit, not for anyone else's. These doctors are not free, you know. They have work to do. We should go to the appointments that are sent to us.

Man: Bangladeshi focus group

Visiting the optician, dentist and chiropodist

Although many of the men and women from the general and Afro-Caribbean samples saw a chiropodist routinely, participants tended to use the optician and dentist as 'emergency services'; less than a quarter of participants overall were having regular check-ups. Apart from people with diabetes or a history of glaucoma in the family, few participants perceived opticians and dentists as 'health professionals' who could recognise the onset of medical conditions in other parts of the body.

Most of the participants in the general and Afro-Caribbean samples had lost all their teeth or had only a few remaining. Thus, they did not feel it was necessary to see a dentist unless they had acute pain or needed new dentures; many people took the view that, at their age, if they had no pain and could still eat, it was best to 'leave well alone'. However, researchers observed that many participants' dentures interfered with speech and appeared to be ill-fitting; when asked, some people in interviews admitted that their dentures were made over 50 years ago. Likewise, if participants could see to read, watch television or drive, with or without spectacles, they did not perceive the need to visit an optician routinely. In addition, many participants in the general and Afro-Caribbean samples were deterred from making regular visits to the dentists and optician by the high cost of check-ups, treatment and new glasses and dentures. This was less of a deterrent for participants on high incomes or those in receipt of state benefits whose treatments were subsidised or free of charge. Many frail and house-bound participants found it too difficult or costly to travel to see an optician or dentist; several people felt that dentists and opticians should be prepared to make domiciliary visits in such cases. The popularity of chiropodists might well have been due to their willingness to make house-calls. Participants made the following comments about these issues:

D'you know, I don't think I've been to the dentist since just before the war. The anaesthetic didn't work and it put me off. I wouldn't be able to have one now because of my heart. I can still eat what I pay for, that's all that matters.

Man, 84: General interviews, urban South

Well, I have to go to the optician once a year because I'm diabetic, but I have a lot of trouble getting there. I think they should call on me, knowing my condition.

Man, 85: General interviews, urban North

Among the South Asian participants, only one man was having chiropody treatment; many participants were unaware of the role of chiropodists. Although the majority of the South Asian participants still had a functional set of natural teeth, most visited the dentist only when in pain or not at all. Some people felt that UK dentistry was too expensive and preferred to have treatment or new dentures made when they visited their home country. Likewise, several people had checks with the optician and new spectacles made abroad.

I have never visited the dentist before in my life.

Woman, 59: Bangladeshi interviewee

I have only been once to the dentists and that was to have my tooth out. My glasses I have had made up from Pakistan. But I tell you, I keep getting appointment cards from that dentist now and I just tear them up and throw them away. The dentists and opticians in this country are so expensive. What's the point?

Woman, 64: Pakistani interviewee

What's the point? Your teeth naturally fall out, don't they, when you are old? I had a friend who went to the dentists in this country, and he ended up being in more pain than when he went in. He did not stop bleeding. When teeth are as old as ours are, they should be left alone. If they are moved, it is likely that they will never settle again.

Man: Bangladeshi focus group

5   Sources of information about healthy behaviour

Apart from issues of diet and nutrition, participants had varying degrees of knowledge and understanding of health-related matters. In general, younger men and women were better informed about health and medical matters than participants aged 75+. Although there were some differences between the South Asian sample and the general and Afro-Caribbean samples, participants felt that they had acquired information in a number of ways, that is, through practice and life experience; by passively absorbing information from medical practitioners, friends, relatives and the media; and by actively seeking advice and information for themselves. Participants were more inclined to seek information for themselves if they had a new or existing medical condition. Furthermore, they were more inclined to ask medical practitioners and nurses for advice and information during 'well-person' checks than when they went to the surgery for other reasons. A number of people said that they occasionally take leaflets from stands in their GP's waiting room, or in the local pharmacy, while others enjoyed reading magazines from private health insurers, such as BUPA, and from support groups, for example, *Balance* published by the British Diabetic Association:

Leaflets, really, I collect leaflets. Anything to do with health, whether it be out of a book . . . and my daughter being a nurse, I often discuss different things, different ailments that other people have, and we compare the way we feel and she makes suggestions.   Man: Afro-Caribbean focus group

While participants from the general and Afro-Caribbean samples saw the press and media as a major source of health information, they nevertheless expressed a high degree of cynicism and mistrust towards this medium. This issue is discussed in Chapter 6. In comparison, members of the South Asian sample generally had a high degree of trust in media items presented in their own languages, for example, radio and satellite or cable television programmes about health, and articles in newspapers printed in the UK and overseas. Major sources of health information for the general and Afro-Caribbean samples were the weekly 'health pages' in newspapers, television dramas and documentaries, such as 'Casualty' and 'Jimmy's', and day-time magazine programmes. However, these were not mentioned by any of the South Asian participants, many of whom were unable to speak English fluently, and were non-literate in English and their own languages.

In general, South Asian participants preferred to receive medication rather than health and lifestyle advice from medical practitioners. Thus, for many of the Bangladeshi, Pakistani and Indian participants, their main sources of health information were family members, friends and spiritual advisers. However, although the 'word-of-mouth' method of transmitting information allowed for discussion of the issues involved, it did mean that there were a number of 'gatekeepers' involved, any of whom might take it upon themselves to censor vital information about potentially embarrassing topics of a sexual or intimate nature. For example, one woman reported that when she asked her grandson to explain a leaflet about breast cancer, he told her that she 'didn't want to know about all that'. South Asian participants made the following comments about their sources of health information:

My family and friends will be where I first get my information from about health and diet and all the new drugs.   Man, 72: Indian interviewee

The most important source I think are family and then your own experience . . . I think your own experiences, and experience of individuals passed down from generation to generation is more valuable than anything . . . It is my son who tells me what is going on with this mad cows' disease . . .

Woman, 66: Pakistani interviewee

I don't think I have enough confidence in anyone other than my immediate family and some close friends. Health is a very important issue. I can't just rely on anyone for information.   Man, 59: Bangladeshi interviewee

Naturally, as you get older you have to take more care of yourself, but with our women that is sometimes difficult to do. I am fortunate, I have caring and educated children. They will tell me what is good for me.

Woman, 56: Pakistani interviewee

6 Deterrents to healthy behaviour

This chapter examines the factors which discouraged the older men and women who took part in the study from actively seeking to promote good health in older age. A number of these factors have been discussed in earlier chapters, for example, the problems caused by the rising cost of transport and paramedical treatment.

The majority of participants were trying not to neglect themselves, or to take too many risks with their health. However, although participants believed they could probably improve their health and wellbeing by taking positive steps to 'behave healthily', relatively few were doing so, and their attempts were often spasmodic. Calnan (1994) makes the following point about health behaviour among people of all ages, which reflects many of the findings of the present study of older people's health beliefs and behaviours:

> '. . . while individual beliefs about health-related behaviors or beliefs about the consequences of the behavior may influence the decision to adopt the behavior in question, social and economic circumstances may provide a setting which can act to enable or constrain the practice of health-related behavior.' Calnan (1994: p. 77)

The data collected in the present study reflect the structural position of older people in UK society, and the social and economic circumstances in which they live. Thus, it was found that the following factors may deter older people from adopting a healthier lifestyle in later life:

- apathy
- the cost of paramedical services
- perceived ageism in the health services
- the perceived lack of credibility of some health information.

Apathy

Younger and able-bodied interviewees were more likely to believe that healthy behaviour could improve health and wellbeing in later life. Thus, interviewees who were taking steps to promote good health tended to be doing so because they believed that they were reducing the risk of certain diseases, because they wanted to enjoy a long and active retirement, and because they believed that it is up to the individual to try to keep himself or herself well. Furthermore, some younger interviewees (55–69) were taking steps to promote good health because they feared the long-term consequences of continuing cut backs in the National Health Service:

We'll be lucky if there's an NHS left by the time we get to 80.

Man, 59: General interviews, rural South

It was such a wonderful idea the NHS, but it's all falling apart now. People have abused it. All these cut backs. There'll be nothing left for the old people at this rate . . .
Woman, 62: General interviews, urban Midlands

In comparison, many older and/or chronically ill interviewees (70+), especially those who felt socially isolated, were apathetic about health-promoting behaviour because they reasoned that they would be dead soon and did not have much future left to worry about. Thus, they did not feel that it was worth bothering to make the effort, especially as irreparable damage had probably been done already. Furthermore, they could not see the point in depriving themselves of 'treats', such as chocolate or a glass of whisky, that made their lives more pleasurable, especially if they lived alone. In a small number of cases, participants felt too physically ill or depressed to make the effort; for example, some participants had so little appetite that they were prepared to eat anything that took their fancy, however 'bad' it was supposed to be for them.

The cost of medical and paramedical treatment

Cost did not deter participants on higher incomes and those in receipt of benefits from seeking medical advice, although those on benefits in rural areas often found it difficult to afford transport to the surgery or hospital. All the participants aged 60 or over were exempt from prescription charges. However, the cost of consulting dentists and opticians prevented a number of participants on low incomes from taking advantage of these services; people on modest incomes tended to use these services for emergencies only. Furthermore, some people who were not entitled to NHS treatment thought that private chiropody was very expensive (for example, £12–£15 in the rural South), although these costs were offset by the willingness of chiropodists to make domiciliary visits so that participants did not have to add on the cost of transport.

Ageism in the health services

Research findings indicate that it is not only the young who may see older people as a burden on the health services, but also some members of the medical profession (Ginn, Arber and Cooper, 1997). In the present study, many participants were deterred from seeking medical advice as a result of both 'internalised ageism' and perceived ageism among health professionals. For example, a large number of participants, especially in the North of England, felt that their doctors saw older people as a 'nuisance', and many participants in the older age groups (70+) expressed concern about going to their GP with problems he or she might dismiss as the inevitable and, therefore, trivial consequences of ageing. Participants made the following comments about this issue:

I don't go any more. I don't want to burden them. These days they're so busy . . .
                                          Woman, 74: General interviews, urban North

I don't like to go . . . I think he might think I'm wasting his time. I worry about what to say, how to explain. Someone who's really bad might need that appointment more than me.   Woman, 76: General interviews, rural North

Whereas many South Asian participants preferred to receive a prescription, men and women from the general and Afro-Caribbean samples wanted medical practitioners to listen to their worries and to offer bereavement counselling; they also wanted GPs in particular to take more interest in the diseases of old age, and to make more effort to understand the day-to-day problems of old age. Participants made the following comments about these issues:

They're not like the old doctors used to be. They're not compassionate. They just stab out tablets. It's in and out, they make you feel rushed. It's awful when you're old.   Woman, 76: General interviews, rural North

My doctor has no time for me. He's too busy. He doesn't understand about old people, their problems. He's not interested, he doesn't listen to me . . .
                                          Man, 85: General interviews, urban Midlands

I would never visit the doctors today about being depressed or worried, only things like a cough. Physical things, not mental things.
                                          Man, 76: General interviews, rural North

My doctor's excellent. He's always got time for me.
                                          Man, 76: General interviews, rural North

Some participants had experienced what they believed to be overt ageism in their dealings with the health services, for example:

I don't like this negative attitude, 'No you can't have that because you're old'. It's an easy cop-out. The doctors say 'You're not 21 any more' . . . I don't expect to be able to run the 4-minute mile but I do object to being patronised.
                                          Man, 76: General interviews, urban North

I've had good and bad experiences of doctors. Some of them have spoken to me like I'm a child, like I'm ignorant. I stood up to one of them once and he treated me better next time.　　　　　　　　　　　Man, 71: General interviews, rural North

Otherwise, it was widely and strongly believed that a sinister form of ageism is operating covertly within both the national and private health services, manifesting as:

- longer waiting lists for degenerative problems of older age, such as hip replacement
- lack of knowledge among health professionals about diseases of older age
- preferential treatment for younger people
- lack of screening for older age groups, such as mammograms
- the withholding of certain treatments
- refusal to treat certain conditions
- a general reluctance to 'waste money' treating older people.

The following comments are representative of many participants' opinions about these issues:

I know more about Parkinson's than my doctor does. I've given him information about it, leaflets, books. It makes you wonder, doesn't it? How can they diagnose something if they don't know anything about it?　　　　Man, 67: rural South

It's frustrating watching the calendar, getting into a worse and worse situation. It could be that younger people are being put to the top of the list, but my days one by one are as precious as anybody else's . . .

Man, 76: (waiting for hernia operation), rural North

The credibility of information about health matters and food safety

A perceived lack of trustworthy sources of information had led to a widespread cynicism among participants from the general and Afro-Caribbean samples, particularly about the veracity of health and food safety information. In general, participants felt that they are being given too much information; that the information is contradictory and confusing; and that some informants' motives are suspect, that is, motivated by profit rather than concern for health. The following comments represent the views of many participants about these issues:

I don't like television documentaries. I reckon they only tell you what they want you to know. They don't give you all the facts. They're all scaremongers . . .

Woman, 55: General interviews, rural Midlands

I like to find out for myself and make my own mind up. There's too many so-called experts contradicting themselves. They change what they tell you every five minutes.

Man, 77: General interviews, rural Midlands

I pick up stuff from the telly. I don't agree with a lot of it. It's all contradictions and interfering in people's lives . . .

Woman, 75: General interviews, rural South

Research evidence suggests that people who feel confused about how they can stay healthy, and which foods they should eat, are less likely to make positive changes to their health-related behaviours (Ferrini, Edelstein and Barrett-Connor, 1994). In the present study, a large number of participants felt that they were being 'bombarded' with confusing information about health and food safety by the media, the food industry, the health industry, government bodies and the medical profession.

. . . there's so much advice. They all contradict one another. 'It's good', 'it's bad'. Please can you tell them if they're going to send us messages in the papers, on TV, please can we have it accurate or not at all?

Man, 76: General interviews, urban North

In addition, many people felt cynical because over the years they had seen health advice 'turn full circle', so that formerly 'healthy' dairy products were now considered too fatty; 'stodgy', fattening carbohydrates were now essential for health; and too much 'protein rich' meat was now considered bad for health. Furthermore, most participants knew of someone who had practised healthy behaviour yet died young, and of others who had abused their bodies and lived to a 'ripe old age':

Some people seem healthy by accident, or they die suddenly even when they've had this 'perfect lifestyle'. I reckon it's a mixture of luck and how you look after yourself. You know, plenty of fresh air, exercise, sport. Not too much, not going over the top, stopping when you've had enough . . .

Man, 68: General interviews, urban South

Thus, in terms of staying healthy, or improving their health, participants generally felt that it was better to trust to their own common sense and to take most health and food safety advice 'with a pinch of salt'.

7 Discussion and recommendations

The data collected in this study provide valuable information on the health beliefs and behaviour of older people. The study highlights the many factors which older people themselves believe contribute towards both good and ill health. However, the study also emphasises the need for policymakers and health-care providers to recognise that older people are not a homogeneous group. Therefore, differences based on ethnicity, class, geographical location and marital status need to be taken into account when developing policy and health promotion programmes for older people.

Combating social isolation

The findings of the study indicate that the level and nature of service provision for older people varies considerably across the country. Furthermore, social isolation has been shown to have a detrimental effect on health. Therefore, it is recommended that a review of service provision for older people should be undertaken. This would help to identify areas where provision is poor as well as models of good practice. Particular attention should be paid to areas where it is known that there is a high level of social deprivation. Consideration also needs to be given to the financial costs incurred by older people in making use of services.

The findings from the current study support previous research in relation to the possible detrimental effects of retirement on health. Similarly, the findings highlight the positive effects on health of maintaining involvement in social activities. When these factors are viewed within the context of a general rise in the standard of living, which means that people are now living longer, it is important that older people can become involved in activities in their local communities. Consequently it is recommended that voluntary organisations providing services for both the older community and the wider community should ensure that they are providing opportunities for older people to be active within the community.

The findings from the current research suggest that while being a carer can have its rewards, many people feel both isolated and unsupported by the wider community. This in turn can have a detrimental effect on both the physical and mental health of the carer. Therefore it is recommended that there should be a review of existing services for carers, with the aim of extending models of good practice. Also, increasing the emphasis on support groups for carers would provide a focus for support and enable people to share their experiences.

In a similar way more attention should be given to the detrimental effects of bereavement on health. However, this should not be confined to the death of a partner or spouse. The current study endorses the findings of previous research in highlighting the negative consequences that the death of a close friend can have on the health of older people. Support groups for older people who have suffered bereavement would be useful.

All those involved in providing health care and social services to older people need to be made fully aware of the detrimental effect that social isolation can have on the health of older people. Furthermore, the current study identified the winter time as being a particular problem for older people, especially those living in the North, where bad weather may prevent them from leaving their home. Organisations providing services for older people need to be aware of this and review their existing transport policies to see if it is possible to provide more transport so that older people can get out more.

Promoting 'good' health

The degree of control that people feel that they have over their health has been a major focus of the current study. At a positive level the findings from the research suggest that people in the younger age group are more likely to express the belief that they have a degree of responsibility over their own health. This needs to be recognised and promoted in health promotion literature. In contrast, the majority of people in the older age group expressed the belief that they had little control over their health. Analysis of the data suggests that one of the reasons for this is due to strongly held beliefs about the role of medicine and the health professional in our society. Firstly, many people feel that health professionals are responsible for their health and secondly that these professionals should only be visited when people are ill. Hence greater emphasis was placed on cure rather than prevention. This issue needs to be addressed in both policy and practice. For example, GPs and other health professionals need to encourage people to become more involved with their own health and to help them to take more control and responsibility. The relationship between doctor and patient needs to be viewed as a partnership in which decisions are made jointly.

The findings from the current study suggest that people are less likely to make changes in their health-related behaviour if they feel they are receiving contradictory or confusing information. This point has particular relevance to information relating to diet and nutrition. A unified approach to health promotion would help reduce confusion among older people. This could be achieved by means of collaboration between the Health Education Authority, community representatives and agencies such as Age Concern, in order to develop a set of health promotion programmes aimed specifically at older people.

The current study suggests that major sources of information for many people are television programmes and the 'health' sections of daily newspapers. Furthermore, health information which is presented informally – for example in television drama or in general interest programmes – needs to be relevant to ordinary people's lives. It is therefore suggested that steps are taken to ensure that the health information presented in light entertainment programmes on television is as factual as possible. Similarly, the producers of such programmes should be encouraged to include more health-related items and story lines that are relevant to older people.

Many of the people who took part in focus groups in Stage 1 of this study said how much they enjoyed discussing health matters with people of their own age. Day centres and luncheon clubs would be useful venues for a countrywide programme of short talks by trained volunteers or health professionals on different health-related topics, followed by group discussions of the issues involved. This would provide a very useful way of disseminating information and encouraging older people to look at attitudes towards health and health behaviour.

In many areas religious leaders, local peer volunteers and agencies such as Age Concern have initiated health promotion programmes at day centres and luncheon clubs used by older people. However activities vary from region to region, and between rural and urban areas. There is a need to identify and evaluate the wide variety of existing programmes. Collaboration between the Health Education Authority and service providers would allow for the rationalisation of existing programmes and the development of new initiatives.

Research evidence suggests that there is less resistance to health promotion advice if it is given by people whose personal characteristics are similar to their audience in terms, for example, of age, ethnicity, gender and class. In some areas, peer advisers have been recruited and trained to give health promotion information to older people, but this type of voluntary activity varies from region to region. Thus, there is a need to identify and evaluate existing peer adviser initiatives, and for the Health Education Authority to advise voluntary agencies on the recruitment and training of older volunteers.

Delivery of health care

The findings suggest that there is a perception amongst older people that the health service is ageist in both attitudes and practices towards older people. This issue needs to be given serious consideration as the results suggest that not only are older people concerned that they will be denied access to scarce health resources, but it also results in a reluctance to seek out medical help. This issue needs to be addressed at all levels of the health service.

Future research

While the current study provides useful information on the health status of older people, its findings are limited by a lack of continuity. Therefore, it is suggested that longitudinal research would provide a more detailed analysis of the changing patterns of older people.

While the current study provides valuable information on older people from ethnic minority groups, the size of the study and the urban location of the participants limit the validity of the findings. Consequently it is suggested that there is a need for more research in this area. In particular this needs to address the issues of older people from ethnic minorities who, through geographical location or social factors, may not have the support of strong community networks.

It has already been acknowledged that the level of service provision is not uniform throughout the country. Therefore a full evaluation of existing social and health-care provision for older people is recommended. This would permit 'models of good practice' to be identified which could then be used to develop policy further.

Research should be undertaken to identify appropriate methods for disseminating health promotion information to older people. In the light of people's dissatisfaction with formal health education literature, such a study could assess the benefits of providing information in different ways, for example peer group discussions and focus groups.

While the current study provides valuable data on the way in which people understand health promotion material, there is a need for more in-depth research in this area. This should consider both general health material and material relating to particular illnesses. Again the use of focus groups and longitudinal studies would be appropriate here for assessing the relevance of health promotion material. This would also have the effect of involving older people more directly in their health, thus encouraging them to take more control over health matters and decisions.

The findings from the current research provide valuable data on general health issues concerning older people. Given that certain illnesses are more common amongst older people, it is recommended that there is a need for research which looks in greater depth at these particular illnesses and their impact on everyday living.

Training

Reference has already been made to the need for further training for those providing health and social services to older people. In the light of this, research examining health professional training in relation to the needs of older people is recommended.

References

Antonovsky, A (1984). In Sidell, M (1995). *Health in Old Age: Myth, Mystery and Management*. Buckingham: Open University Press.

Arber, S and Ginn, J (1991) *Gender and Later Life: a Sociological Analysis of Resources and Constraints*. London: Sage.

Arber, S and Ginn, J (eds) (1995) *Connecting Gender and Ageing: a Sociological Approach*. Buckingham: Open University Press.

Bhopal, R S (1986) 'The inter-relationship of folk, traditional and Western medicine within an Asian community in Britain', *Social Science and Medicine* **22**(1): 99–105.

Blaxter, M (1990) *Health and Lifestyles*. London: Tavistock-Routledge.

Blaxter, M (1995) 'What is health?' In Davey, B, Gray, A and Seale, C (eds) (1995) *Health and Disease: a Reader*. Buckingham: Open University Press.

Calnan, M (1987) *Health and Illness: the Lay Perspective*. London: Tavistock.

Calnan, M (1990) 'Food and health'. In Cunningham-Burley, S and McKegney, N (eds) (1990) *Readings in Medical Sociology*. London: Tavistock.

Calnan, M (1994) '"Lifestyle" and its social meaning', *Advances in Medical Sociology* **4**: 69–87.

Calnan, M and Williams, S (1991) 'Style of life and the salience of health', *Sociology of Health and Illness* **4**: 506–29.

Choudry, S (1996) *Pakistani Women and Domestic Violence*, Home Office Research Findings No. 43. London: Home Office Research and Statistics Directorate.

Ferrini, R, Edelstein, S and Barrett-Connor, E (1994) 'The association between health beliefs and health behavior change in older adults', *Preventive Medicine* **23**(1): 1–5.

Giddens, A (1997) *Sociology*. 3rd edition. Cambridge: Polity Press.

Ginn, J, Arber, S and Cooper, H (1997) *Researching Older People's Health Needs and Health Promotion Issues*. London: Health Education Authority.

Graham, H (1987) 'Being poor'. In Branner, J and Wilson, G *Give and Take in Families: Studies of Resource Distribution*. London: Allen & Unwin.

Greenhalgh, T, Helman, C and Chowdhury, A M (1998) 'Health beliefs and folk models of diabetes in British Bangladeshis: a qualitative study', *British Medical Journal* **316**: 978–83.

Grimley Evans, J (1994) 'Can we live to be a healthy hundred?' *MRC News*, autumn, No. 64: 18–21.

Grundy, E (1994) 'Live old, live well', *MRC News*, autumn, No. 64: 22–5.

Hunt, S and McLeod, M (1987) cited in Calnan, M (1994) '"Lifestyle" and its social meaning', *Advances in Medical Sociology* **4**: 69–87.

Jerrome, D (1986) 'Me Darby, you Joan'. In Phillipson, C, Bernard, M and Strang, P (eds) (1986) *Dependency and Interdependency in Old Age: Theoretical Perspectives and Policy Alternatives*. London: Croom Helm in association with the British Society of Gerontology.

OPCS (1996) *Population Trends 86*. London: HMSO.

Sidell, M (1995) *Health in Old Age: Myth, Mystery and Management*. Buckingham: Open University Press.

Walker, A and Maltby, T (1997) *Ageing Europe*. Buckingham: Open University Press.